THE
COOKALONG
BOOK

THE COOKALONG BOOK

by

Barbara
Wyden

DAVID McKAY COMPANY, INC.
New York

THE COOKALONG BOOK

Book design by C. R. Bloodgood

LIBRARY OF CONGRESS CATALOG CARD NUMBER: 79-188261
MANUFACTURED IN THE UNITED STATES OF AMERICA

CONTENTS

Come Cook with Me   1
How to Use the Cookalong Book:
    A Baker's Dozen of Suggestions   8
Note to the Senior Cook   21
Note to the Junior Cook   23

MORNING, NOON AND NIGHT

One   A Baker's Dozen of Good Mornings   27
    Alarm Clock Bacon   27
    Friendly Eggs   29
    Parlez-Vous French Toast?   31

Pancakes, Plain and Fancy   33
    Basic Flapjacks   33
    Fruity Flapjacks   35
    Meaty Griddle Cakes   36
    Flying Saucer Pancake   37
    Ben's Eatemallup Muffins (and Muffins-
      in-Disguise)   39, 41
    Cornflake Cake (Yes, Cornflake Cake!)   41
    Oatmeal, Yecch!   44
    Oatburgers   45
    Lazy Lucy's Wake-up Rice   46
    Glop on Toast   48

Two   A Baker's Dozen of Lunchtime Specials   51

Macaroni and You-Know-What   52
BLT on Toast   54
Phony Pizza   55
Ken's Double Feature   56
Canny Casserole   57
Basic Chicken Soup   59
Sally's Prize-Winning Chicken Salad   62
Tomato Hideaway   64

Ho Ho, Ho Ho, It's Off to School We Go!   66
Lunch Box Superspecials   66

The Energy Special   66
Peanut-Butter-and-Jelly What?   67

Linda's Diet Lunches   68

Mustard (Uh-huh) Sandwiches   68
Ketchup (Yup) Sandwiches   69
Apple (Why Are You Laughing?)
Sandwiches   69

**Three   A Baker's Dozen of Things to Cook for
Dinner (or Supper) as the Case May Be   71**

Jeff's Messy Macaroni   72
Basic Spaghetti   73
Spaghetti and Meatballs   75
Sam's Chicken Chunks   77
Katy's Throw-Everything-in Meat Loaf   78
Susan's French Beef Stew   79
Second-Helping Pot Roast   81
Basic Roast Beef   84
Skinny Potatoes   86
Fancy Baked Potatoes   87
Beginner's Basic Salad Kit   88
Good Old Spinach   90
Hot Buttered Juice   92

SUMMER AND WINTER

Four **A Baker's Dozen of Summer Coolers and**
Vacation Projects   **95**

L-o-b-s-t-e-r Spells Summer	95
Green and Yellow Sauce	97
Billion-Dollar Lobster Roll	98
Dippy Shrimp	100
Pete's Tower of Pisa	101
Grate Chicken	103
Caveman Steak	104
There's Potato Salad	105
Sixteen-Minute Blueberry Cheesecake	107
Crumbly Pie Crust	109
Shivering Cold Lemonade	110
Muscleman Bread	111
Your Own Homemade Strawberry Jam	117

Five **A Baker's Dozen of Winter Warmers**
and Treats   **120**

Boilaway Beef	120
Pickled Buddy Sauce	123
Hot and Cold Sauce	123
Historical Beans	124
Wild West Beans	126
Johnnycake	127
Third-Generation Lasagne	128
Spicy Gingerbread	130
Whipped Cream	132
Apple Lollypops	133
Pully-Tuggy Taffy	134
Snow Bowl	136
Chocolate Survival Kit	137

HAPPY DAYS AND HOLIDAYS

Six **A Baker's Dozen of Celebrations**   **141**

        Once-Upon-a-Birthday Cake   **141**
        Cranky Ice Cream   **145**
        Chanukah Seedy Cookies   **149**

Christmas Is Delicious   **150**

    Decorations Good Enough to Eat   **150**

        Popcorn Balls   **150**
        Gingerbread Men and Women and Stars
           and Wreaths, et cetera and Frosting **152, 154**

Tasty Presents   **156**

    For Friends and Relatives   **156**
    For Birthday and Hostess and Thank-You
        and Christmas and Surprise Gifts   **156**
    For Just-Because-I-Like-You Presents   **156**

        Green Cheese Balls   **157**
        Peaches in a Basket   **159**
        Your Own Pâté Maison   **163**
        Holiday Bird   **165**

Fishermen's Picnic Basket   **167**

        First Catch Your Fish   **168**
        Campfire Potatoes   **169**
        Onions, Hooray!   **170**
        Foiled Again Corn   **171**
        P.S. And to Wash It All Down   **172**
        P.P.S. How to Turn the Fishermen's Picnic
           Basket into a Skaters' or a Skiers' or
           a Tobogganers' Picnic Basket . . . Any
           Old Kind of Picnic Basket   **172**

GOURMET COOKING AND MENUS

Seven So Now You're a Junior Gourmet:
A Baker's Dozen of Gourmet Recipes   175

The Armadillo Vegetable   176
Lovable Asparagus   177
Rice with an Italian Accent   178
Veal Chops in an Envelope   179
Beef with a Russian Accent   181
Flaky Pie Crust   183
Cheese and Onion Pie   186
Light as a Feather Cheese Soufflé   188
New England Apple Pie   190
Strawberries Romanoff   192
Meringues   194
Ice Cream Whirligig   195
Superchocolate Nut Sauce   197

PUTTING IT ALL TOGETHER

Eight A Baker's Dozen of Cookalong Menus   201

A Sunday Breakfast   202
Let's Surprise Mother with Breakfast in Bed   202
An All-American Sunday Dinner   202
A Week Night Supper for the Family   203
A Good Company Dinner   203
A Gourmet Feast   203
A Buffet Supper   204
A Cold-Weather Saturday Night Supper,
     New England Style   204
When It's 90 Degrees in the Shade   204
The Team's Coming Over for a Cookout   204

All My Best Friends Are Coming for a
Slumber Party   205
  Slumber Party Supper   205
  A Midnight (and Later) Snack   205
  A Brunch for the Morning After   205

The End   206

Index   207

THE
COOKALONG
BOOK

COME COOK WITH ME

Father rushes out most mornings after a swift gulp of coffee. The children force down their cold cereal standing at the kitchen counter. And mother wearily drinks her second cup of coffee in solitary squalor among the debris of hasty breakfasts—unless, she, too, has to dash out to her job. In the evening, homework, social engagements, meetings and community obligations propel parents and children along separate paths. The leisurely give-and-take between parent and child at mealtimes—once comfortably taken for granted—has almost disappeared.

Paradoxically, the pressures—and the pleasures—of the world outside the home have narrowed rather than enriched children's lives. Even the most affluent young are becoming emotionally impoverished, deprived of the love, the protection, the nurturing that are the fabric of family life. The family is abdicating its role as model for the young. More and more, the job is left to the community, the schools, the distortions of television, to other youngsters, to God-knows-who-or-what. And as the generations drift apart, some psychologists are actually predicting the extinction of family life as we know it.

What has all this to do with a cookbook? It happens to be the *raison d'être* for this one. *The Cookalong Book* was created to help parents and children rediscover the fun of being a family, to draw the generations closer together. This book won't work if you hand it to a child. It's designed for parent *and* child, grandparent *and* grandchild, big sister *and* little brother, aunt *and* nephew. So it's really more than a book, it's a doing. And I hope it will open the door to the creative world of cooking for boys and girls (and parents, too).

Since when, you may ask, is cooking creative? It always has been. What could be more creative than starting out with seemingly unrelated ingredients and winding up with a neatly blended (and tasty) dish? What better way is there to show a child that he or she (her/his skill, his/her patience, her/his taste, his/her judgment) can make a real difference? And what better teaching tool could you find than food—something that everyone enjoys and no one can dismiss as unimportant? And what better way to establish sensible health habits and, yes, even just demonstrate a few realities that are rapidly getting lost in the shuffle of today's artificialities?

Many children don't even know how real food tastes. If a dish doesn't contain a dash of monosodium glutamate, a pinch of sodium phosphate, a sprinkle of BHT (whatever that is) to "preserve quality," a little calcium propionate to retard spoilage, and some artificial flavoring, well, it just doesn't taste like home cooking to them.

I can see the cookbooks of the future now. They're going to read like chemical formulas. Pantry shelves will be stocked with jars of sodium this and that, bottles of mono- and di-glycerides, more and more sophisticated flavor enhancers and spoilage retarders—and less and less sugar and spice and everything nice (and real). And there will be all sorts of computer-controlled staples—

scrambled egg pellets, roast beef powder, lamb chop flakes and (heaven help us!) dehydrated hamburgers with artificial ketchup.

That dreary chemical day is still in the future, hopefully an avoidable future. While children do enjoy the most awful glop (like frozen cardboard pizza and those worthless sugar-coated cereals), it's only because they aren't exposed to the better tastes of life.

I became convinced of this one winter afternoon a few years ago. We had gone ice-skating with two young visitors, Caroline, five, and Eleanor, nine. When we came home, I made hot chocolate, starting from scratch with bitter chocolate squares. We drank it with small mountains of whipped cream floating on top—cream whipped before the children's eyes. They were startled and fascinated. They thought you made hot chocolate by adding water to some powder and that whipped cream came from a gas-activated pressure can. (If you're tempted by the idea of rich hot chocolate, you'll find the Chocolate Survival Kit in the Baker's Dozen of Winter Warmers. And the whipped cream, too.)

Then I made an apple pie for supper. Caroline and Eleanor were enchanted. They had never seen anyone roll out pie crust. I showed them how to arrange the apple slices and let them sprinkle on the sugar and cinnamon. They rolled out the leftover pastry to make their own small apple turnovers. Well, you never saw such enthusiastic lip-smacking! Part of their enjoyment came from the good spicy apple taste and the flaky crust (New England Apple Pie and Flaky Pie Crust are on pages 190 and 183.); most of it, though, came from their pride of accomplishment, their sense of participation, the satisfaction of creating.

When their parents came to pick them up after supper, the girls were bubbling. Caroline boasted, "We made homemade cooking! And we ate it all!"

The next day their mother telephoned. "Caroline and Eleanor haven't stopped talking about the great time they had in your kitchen," she reported. "I promised them we could start cooking together on Saturdays. But what'll we make? I don't know where to begin."

That's how *The Cookalong Book* was born. It started as a listing of simple recipes for Eleanor and Caroline. Soon I realized that very few everyday American dishes are beyond the competence of a young cook—provided mother is right on hand with advice (tactful, of course) and assistance (only when requested or needed). And for safety's sake, too. *Children should not be allowed to work with sharp knives, boiling water, electrical appliances, etc., without careful adult supervision until they have acquired the necessary judgment and competence.*

The secret, I discovered through testing, is simple and explicit instructions—written almost as part of a dialogue between cook and book.

The Cookalong Book offers no magic formula for instant intimacy. Cookalong sessions provide only the vital framework—the companionable, unselfconscious atmosphere in which emotional growth and security flourish. A rapport is established that can carry over to other phases of the parent-and-child relationship. Equally important, the stage is set for achievement in many areas outside the kitchen.

When Caroline cooked her first Saturday lunch by herself (well, almost) and her father asked for a second helping, it was one of life's triumphs. (Her menu: Macaroni and You-Know-What from A Baker's Dozen of

Lunchtime Specials and Good Old Spinach from A Baker's Dozen of Things to Cook for Dinner.) Caroline was just one big smile. She couldn't have begun to tell you how pleased and proud she felt, how she basked in her daddy's approval.

For Eleanor, the cookalong sessions helped overcome her shyness in the social world of boys and girls together.

"Eleanor was terribly upset when her friends started having boy-girl parties," her mother told me. "All of a sudden, she turned very shy and awkward.

"But she worked it out for herself. When her birthday came around, she asked if she could have a cookalong party. She had it all planned out. They would make chicken salad. And they'd make the birthday cake and frost it themselves.

"The party was a great success. She invited three boys and two other girls. (Eleanor's menu consisted of Sally's Prize-Winning Chicken Salad from A Baker's Dozen of Lunchtime Specials and Once-Upon-a-Birthday Cake from A Baker's Dozen of Happy Days and Holidays.) The kitchen was crowded and noisy and everyone had a marvelous time. Especially Eleanor. She seemed to have forgotten that she was ever uncomfortable with boys.

"And there was an extra dividend," Eleanor's mother added. "Ever since, we usually have a boy or two cooking along with us on Saturdays."

Some parents have an uneasy feeling that the kitchen is no place for boys, that only sissies would be interested in cooking. They couldn't be more mistaken. Cooking gives boys as well as girls a sense of competence. Each culinary success helps bolster self-esteem. And they get as much fun out of it as they do from making model airplanes or messing around with chemistry sets.

Ron and Jeff Wyden received an extra dose of self-esteem one long-ago Sunday morning. The men of the family were on their own and their breakfast plans were ambitious. Bacon and eggs *and* pancakes. Jeff fried the bacon. Ron stirred up the pancakes. And their father was the scrambled eggs chef. He used too much butter, turned the heat up too high and didn't stir enough. According to reliable reports, the scrambled eggs were a disaster. But the boys thoroughly enjoyed daddy's cheerful culinary incompetence. After ten years, daddy's scrambled eggs still elicit a good-humored groan when it's reminiscence time.

I've had my own kitchen comedowns. One summer when we were vacationing on Martha's Vineyard, I decided to go native. I sent the boys out to pick blueberries and flipped through my good Bostonian *Fanny Farmer Cookbook* for a truly New England recipe. I settled on Cape Cod Blueberry Grunt, which was described as "an old-fashioned treat" and certainly sounded authentic.

As I mixed the biscuit dough to cover the blueberries, I enthused over how good it was going to be, "just the kind of food the early settlers ate." The boys watched dubiously as I put "that mess" in the oven.

They were even more dubious when I put dessert on the table. It was a sorry sight. It sank in the middle. It was oyster white on top instead of toasty brown. And inside—a soggy mass of half-baked biscuit and blueberries.

Ron exclaimed, "What do you call that? Blueberry Slump?"

Ever since, my cooking has been rated on a Blueberry-Slump scale—"worse than Blueberry Slump" or "better than Blueberry Slump."

The moral of this story? Well, I guess it's "courage." And also that failures don't matter. It's the involvement that counts.

Family traditions, those intangibles that bind the generations together, are made up of thousands of things, including even inedible scrambled eggs and Blueberry Slump. And, perhaps, parental disasters of this kind help children see their parents as fallible human beings—just like themselves.

I only wish now that we had spent more time together in the kitchen when the boys were younger. And I hope that *The Cookalong Book* will encourage parents to do more things with their children—in and out of the kitchen—to garden or paint or listen to music or bicycle or almost anything. You'll have fun and so will they, as long as it's something that can be started without too much fussing and then begins to come naturally. I doubt that any parent could induce a child to enjoy house-cleaning-along-with-mother or lawn-mowing-along-with-father. Such things are chores and must be done and that's all there is to it. But cooking . . . it's really a privilege and a pleasure.

So, wash your hands, put on your aprons and let's get started!

HOW TO USE THE COOKALONG BOOK: A BAKER'S DOZEN OF SUGGESTIONS

The Cookalong Book is arranged to work at several levels. The way you use it depends on the age and experience of the Junior Cook or Cooks. The following suggestions will help both Junior and Senior Cooks get the most fun and learning out of their cookalong sessions.

1. WHERE DO WE START?

Start at the very beginning of the book with the Baker's Dozen of Good Mornings and cook your way right through to So Now You're a Junior Gourmet. You can skip some of the recipes, but follow the general plan.

To the Junior Cook:

You may ask, "Who wants to cook a baker's dozen of breakfasts?" Well, if you will read the Good Morning recipes carefully, you'll see that most of them can be eaten for lunch or dinner just as well as for breakfast. French toast and bacon are a good Sunday night supper. Eatemallup Muffins are a welcome addition to any meal. A Flying Saucer Pancake is a super dessert. So is a Cornflake Cake. And so on.

To the Senior Cook:

It's not only logical to start at the beginning; it's also more practical. The recipes are carefully arranged so that the fledgling cook acquires basic cooking skills in easy stages. The first chapter is designed to help a youngster feel confident in the kitchen—to use the frying pan, the double boiler, the oven. Children will learn how to cook rice, break eggs and make a cream sauce. Each skill is used again and again in more sophisticated ways in following chapters. For instance, when the Junior Cook learns to make the cream sauce for Glop (chipped beef) on Toast, he/she has acquired a technique that she/he can use again to make a macaroni-and-cheese casserole or a gourmet specialty like a soufflé. And by the time the young cook comes to the sophisticated recipes at the end of the book, he/she can take them in stride, because the basic techniques are all familiar.

2. WHEN DO WE START?

The best time to start is the day before. Choose your recipe. Read it through. See if you have everything in the kitchen that you'll need. If not, add the necessary items to your shopping list.

3. HOW DO WE START?

To the Senior Cook:

If the Junior Cook is eight years old or under, it's a good idea to read the recipe as a bedtime story the night before. Discuss just what you'll both be doing the next day. Talk about the directions and explain them a little. Perhaps you can plan the rest of the meal together. If you read these recipes with warmth and interest, your beginner cook will be amused, beguiled and eager for tomorrow to come.

No matter what the age of the Junior Cook, the day-before discussion period can be a constructive experience. You might say, "Now, let's see. What time should we start cooking if we want to have Messy Macaroni for supper tomorrow?" Let the Junior Cook read over the recipe again and make an estimate. Or say, "If you're making lasagne for tomorrow night, perhaps I should make the dessert. What do you think would be good?" Then the two of you can leaf through this book, or choose a recipe from another cookbook. The point is involvement, getting the younger cook interested in planning a meal and pleasing the family.

To the Junior Cook:

As soon as you learn how to read, it might be a good idea for *you* to read the recipe out loud to the Senior Cook. Talk about what you'd like to do. For instance, if you're planning to make Fruity Flapjacks for breakfast, it's a good idea to decide the day before just what kind of fruit you want to use. You may need to make a trip to the store.

4. HOW OLD DOES A JUNIOR COOK HAVE TO BE?

Old enough to be interested. Many children will ask if they can help. Others indicate interest by pretending to cook when they're playing. Don't rush a child into cooking.

To the Senior Cook:

You know your own child, her/his muscular coordination, his/her attention span. Cooking isn't an overnight achievement. Let the child get involved in easy stages. Let your toddler pour her/his own pancake on the griddle (under your eagle-eyed supervision, of course). Let your preschooler make a tiny turnover with leftover piecrust and a handful of apple slices. Let the children cut out a few cookies or help frost a couple of cupcakes. They'll take forever and make a mess, but they'll love it. This is the way competence is created. Slowly. And with enjoyment.

A four-year-old is probably old enough to start joining in cookalong sessions. But don't expect too much. And don't scold when attention wanders. You'll almost certainly discover that each small culinary triumph whets the appetite for another cooking session.

5. WHAT'S THE BEST TIME TO HAVE A COOKALONG SESSION?

Whenever you feel like it. During the school year, Saturday morning might be the best time. Or Friday afternoons. During vacations, well, just set a mutually agreeable time. The main thing is to have a clear block of time. And a minimum of outside distractions.

To the Senior Cook:
Don't plan a cookalong when you're tired. Fatigue leads to impatience and crankiness.

To the Junior Cook:
Cooking is a lot of fun. And it's a privilege, too. But don't say yes to a cookalong just to be agreeable. If you'd rather be out riding your bicycle or you feel more like reading, well then, say so. But think twice before saying no. You usually have a pretty good time cooking, don't you?

6. HOW MUCH HELP SHOULD YOU GIVE? OR GET?

To the Senior Cook:

If you're cooking along with a four-year-old, you'll have to do most of the work, but, preferably, without seeming to. A four-year-old will forgive you cheerfully for doing all the hard parts as long as you do them unobtrusively, as long as he/she knows that she/he did some work and as long as you leave him/her to take pride in the finished product.

That's not as tricky as you might think. Let the preschooler measure out ingredients. Discuss measurements with the small cook. Explain the differences between teaspoons and tablespoons. Show how many teaspoons make a tablespoon. A preschooler can add ingredients to a bowl, can stir, can butter pans. With proper supervision, he/she can even chop a slice or two of onion, break an egg into the meat loaf mixture, all sorts of things. It may take all afternoon to make a batch of cookies. Or the limit of the Junior Cook's attention span may be reached in half an hour. Don't force it. For the youngest cooks, especially, the kitchen experience should be one of fun, of achievement and of feeling grown-up. Once you've seen the pride on a four- or five-year-old's face as he flips his first pancake or she fills baked potato shells with mashed potato for Sunday dinner, then you'll understand just why cooking along is so satisfying for both parent and child. Give the child as much responsibility as possible. Be generous with your praise. And eat the results of the cookalong with obvious pleasure.

The middle-aged child (oh, from seven to ten) is quite competent. The Senior Cook can cook one dish and let the Junior Cook prepare another. Talk about what you're doing, so the youngster can share in your experience too. Try not to hover or boss. An alert eye will enable the Senior Cook to spot and quietly avert most catastrophes. When the Junior Cook is aware that you're busy about your own recipe, she/he will feel more relaxed. And for heaven's sake, don't insist that the beginner do everything properly. It takes time and practice to acquire competence, remember? Give advice when asked and try to keep hands off as much as possible.

From ten years old and up, depending on how much kitchen know-how a child has accumulated, it's pretty clear sailing. These youngsters have the brains and the muscular control to tackle almost everything. There may be times when he or she will want to have the kitchen to himself or herself. And that's fine. But don't let the child's competence take the fun out of cooking. Don't turn it into a chore just because eleven-year-old Julie or Bob can get supper alone. That's *not* the point of *The Cookalong Book.*

To the Junior Cook:

Ask your mother or father for help when you're not sure what to do. And ALWAYS ASK FOR HELP when you see instructions in capital letters in this book. They're there for a purpose. Most of them are like a warning signal that says "THIS *COULD BE DANGEROUS* IF YOU DON'T DO IT PROPERLY."

Please be sure to ask questions about everything you don't understand. And if you feel that your mother or father is doing too much of the cooking on your recipe, well then, speak up. Let them know how you feel. Even the greatest parent is not a mind reader.

And don't, please don't, ever cook something in a cook-

along session that you don't feel like cooking. There is a
time for chores and there is a time for fun. Cookalongs
are for fun. Sometimes your mother may ask you to help
get dinner or make lunch. Well, then, whether you really
feel like it or not, you should do it—and do it cheerfully.
But cookalong sessions should be something else. They're
for the fun of doing something with your mother and
father, for doing things together, for having a good time.
So don't get the two things mixed up. If you don't, then
your parents won't either.

7. WHO DOES WHAT?

You'll have to decide where to draw this line for your-
selves. A lot depends on the age of the Junior Cook. As a
rule of thumb, the younger cook should do as much as
possible.

To the Senior Cook:

Please be safety conscious. The kitchen can be dangerous. Please be on hand when your child is handling hot
water and hot fat. Please supervise when the oven or
broiler or stove-top burners are being turned on. Be sure
he/she has a good supply of sturdy pot holders. Explain
that damp pot holders or wet cloths should never be used
to pick up hot pans or utensils.

Please teach the fledgling cook how to peel, to chop, to
slice. And above all, make sure that your novice has good
sharp knives to work with. You do know (don't you?)
that the sharper the knife the safer. Dull, blunt knives are
accident-provokers. When the cook has to exert extra
pressure to make a dull knife cut, there's more chance of
the knife slipping and cutting the cook rather than the
food. Yes, sharp knives *are* also dangerous. But if a child
is taught to use knives properly, to take care of them and

respect them, their danger potential is pretty well dulled.

Children must be taught—and you will undoubtedly have to demonstrate over and over—the proper techniques of cutting and chopping. If the Senior Cook lacks knife know-how, *Mastering the Art of French Cooking* by Beck, Bertholle and Child has an excellent chapter on cutting, chopping, slicing, dicing and mincing that explains and illustrates the correct way to hold knives and use them. (I disagree with these authors' recommendation that knives be stored in a magnetic wall holder. This is too dangerous when young children are learning their way around the kitchen. Knives are too easily knocked off these magnetic holders. I prefer a wooden knife rack where each knife can be inserted securely.)

The Junior Cook should be taught to regard knives as important tools, just as carpenters and surgeons regard the tools of their trades. The youngsters should learn to wash, dry and put away a knife the instant they are through with it.

Please make sure that the Junior Cook does not use the oven, the broiler, electric mixer, blender or any other electrical, hot or sharp-edged helper without supervision. Obviously, there will come a time when you are confident of the Junior Cook's ability. Then you can grant permission to "solo." But until then, keep a sharp (but not too, too obvious) eye on things.

Please try not to be *over*protective. Don't employ scare tactics or turn the kitchen into a frightening place. I know it's difficult, but as long as you're on hand and watching carefully, nothing much will go wrong. And keep in mind that gentle reminders about the correct way to chop and slice are far more effective—and safer—than sudden shrieks of "Be careful!"

8. WHY SHOULD I TEACH MY SON TO COOK?

Why not? He eats, doesn't he? So why not teach him the fundamentals of cookery, a pursuit that the great French chef Carême ranked as one of the fine arts along with painting, music and sculpture.

To the Senior Cook:

Too many parents, fathers especially, tend to think of cooking as woman's work. They feel there's something effeminate about a boy knowing his way around the kitchen. Well, there isn't. The greatest chefs in the world, almost without exception, have been men. (Today a good chef is paid substantially more than the average lawyer, accountant or salesman.)

And there are some very persuasive reasons for a boy to know how to cook. For instance, a boy who understands the skill, the care, the thought and the energy involved in preparing meals will have a greater appreciation and respect for "woman's work."

To the Junior Cook:

If any of your friends should be so stupid as to say cooking is for sissies, don't bother to beat him up. Just feel sorry for him. A kid who says that is probably—way deep down—afraid that *he* has a bit of sissy in him.

Boys should know enough about cooking to scramble eggs, make hamburgers and take care of themselves in emergencies. That's the minimum. If you get really interested in cooking, there are a lot of good cookbooks written by men that you might ask your parents to get for you after you've cooked your way through this book.

9. SHOULD FATHERS COOKALONG WITH DAUGHTERS?

Of course. It's a wonderful chance for fathers and daughters to do something together.

To the Junior Cook:

Your father may not be very experienced in the kitchen so be sure you explain about reading the recipes through, checking to see if you have the ingredients and planning your time before you start cooking. He'll be proud of how much you know.

To the Senior Cook:

You realize, don't you, that you're engaged in much more than cooking. You're showing your daughter that men as well as women experience pride and pleasure in creating a dish and in showing love in the most basic way—feeding the ones you hold dear.

Respect your daughter's competence in the kitchen. Don't turn her into a cook's helper. Share the drudgery and the fun.

10. HOW MANY PEOPLE SHOULD COOKALONG TOGETHER?

Two is usually most satisfactory, the Senior Cook and the Junior Cook. Too many cooks not only spoil the broth, they also make for a lot of confusion. When two or more youngsters are working on different recipes in the same kitchen, a mother has to have the energy of a nuclear reactor, the patience of a saint, a sturdy sense of humor— and at least six hands. But every mother does, doesn't she?

To the Senior Cook:

Cooking along with a child is a marvelous way to establish a mood of intimacy and experience true compan-
ionship. If you have two or more children, each one
should have a chance for individual cookalong sessions. I
know it's hard to arrange the time. But do it anyway. The
reward is worth the effort.

11. WHO DOES THE SHOPPING?

It's a good idea to do it together.

To the Senior Cook:

Preschoolers are not too young to learn a little about
buying food. They'll be interested if they know it's for
something they're going to cook—and eat.

Older children will be interested in learning how to
choose vegetables, how to figure out the best buy in
canned goods, how to buy meat. They usually have a
sound respect for value and enjoy getting the most for
their money.

Older children should be trusted to go shopping alone.
But, a word of warning: Don't be impatient with their
mistakes. We all make them. It's one way of learning.
Explain why a youngster's choice was unwise. Suggest
what would have been a better buy. But don't blame. And
don't scold.

12. DO WE HAVE TO MAKE EVERY
SINGLE RECIPE?

Of course not. There's no point in cooking something
you don't like. Just skip it. Go on to the next recipe.

13. WHAT IF A YOUNGSTER DOESN'T WANT TO COOK?

Don't insist. There are plenty of other rewarding activities that parents and children can enjoy together. But you don't have to take no for an answer right off. See if something comes up that kindles the child's interest. Use your imagination. It might be a good idea to start with Apple Lollypops or a Snow Bowl or Chocolate Survival Kit instead of beginning at the beginning. You can always go back.

Wait for a rainy afternoon and suggest making gingerbread. A child who is almost over a feverish cold but not quite ready to go back to school might get interested in throwing together a meat loaf for dinner.

Some children relish advance planning. Others like spur-of-the-moment projects. Be flexible. Rules are made to be broken. All except this one: COOKALONGS SHOULD BE HAPPY TIMES.

p.s. and who cleans up?
BOTH OF YOU!

NOTE TO THE SENIOR COOK

Let me confess right here and now that *The Cookalong Book* is woefully lacking in recipes for liver and carrots and lamb and kidneys and turnips and parsnips. For tapioca pudding and pumpkin pie. And squash. And many other foods that are "good for you." Or so they say.*

The choice of recipes reflects not only my own preferences, but those of the children who, over the years, have taught me what they'll gobble up and what they'll leave on their plates.

* If your child clamors to learn how to mash turnips or broil a tasty bit of liver, why then it's easy enough to jot down directions on a three-by-five cookalong file card for your youngster's private cookalong collection of recipes.

NOTE TO THE
JUNIOR COOK

Do you know what a baker's dozen is? It's twelve—plus one more for good measure. In the old days, when people went to the bakery shop, the kind of place that had a big black stove in the back where the baker and his wife baked all sorts of good-smelling breads and pies and cakes and cookies, a baker's dozen was a sign of generosity. A generous measure.

When you would ask for "a dozen doughnuts, please," the baker's wife would count the spicy smelling doughnuts (sometimes they were still warm) into a brown paper bag. She'd say, "One . . . two . . . three . . . four . . . five . . . six . . . seven . . . eight . . . nine . . . ten . . . eleven and twelve. One dozen. And one more for good measure." That's a baker's dozen.

I've always thought a baker's dozen was a good measure for almost anything. It's the one extra effort, the one extra smile, the little bit of giving or trying or caring beyond what you absolutely have to do that makes the difference. That's why there's a baker's dozen of everything in these cookalong chapters. In fact, I'll tell you a secret. Sometimes there's even more, because there were so many things I wanted to tell you about.

And now, my wish for you is that you have a baker's dozen of a baker's dozen of good times in the kitchen with your family and your friends.

MORNING, NOON AND NIGHT

ONE

A BAKER'S DOZEN
of
GOOD MORNINGS

Mornings are beginnings. When you wake up you never know what good experiences lie ahead. But you can make sure of one—and that's breakfast. What makes a good breakfast? Good food and good company, of course. The family that turns breakfast into a series of solitary snacks is missing part of the fun of being a family. It's up to you cooks—both Junior and Senior—to make breakfast a meal the whole family will want to share—especially on weekends. The recipes in this chapter should start you off on the right foot (or should I say "on the right side of bed"?).

ALARM CLOCK BACON

Bacon is the best alarm clock ever. Even on the coldest morning when everyone is asleep, all snuggled under the blankets, once they smell bacon frying, they're wide awake and hungry.

Bacon is good with eggs and pancakes and French

toast and in sandwiches and salad. In fact, once you've learned to fry bacon right, you're on your way to becoming a really good cook.

Here's how you start.

First, read the recipe all the way through. You should *always* do that with *every* recipe. Then tie on your apron, wash your hands, and count out:

> 3 pieces of bacon for each person (Some people might like more.)

1. Get out the big black iron frying pan and put it on the stove.

2. Separate the bacon strips and place them neatly in the cold frying pan. Now turn on the heat. Keep it low. (If the bacon is icy cold, don't try to separate it into strips. Just figure out how much you'll need and put it in the cold frying pan all in one piece. When it gets warm you can separate the pieces very easily. Use two forks to separate them. You'll find using two is easier than one.)

3. Let the bacon cook slowly. When it starts giving off fat, ASK YOUR MOTHER TO HELP YOU POUR IT OFF INTO A CAN. *BE CAREFUL.* YOU CAN GET A BAD BURN FROM HOT FAT.

4. Now turn each strip over carefully with a spatula and a fork or two forks. Try to keep the strips flat. Let them cook (make sure the heat is still low) and turn them a couple more times.

5. When the bacon is nice and brown on both sides, put some paper towels down on the counter. Take the bacon out of the frying pan and put it on the paper towels so that they will absorb all the fat. This makes the bacon nice and crispy.

6. If you're not quite ready to serve breakfast, turn the

oven on to 250 degrees. Put the bacon on some aluminum foil and pop it in the oven until you need it.

FRIENDLY EGGS

The friendliest eggs, of course, are scrambled eggs, because they get along so well with each other. They get along very well with bacon, too. Scrambled eggs and bacon are a very friendly way to start the day.

First you get together:

> Eggs (You need 1 egg for each person and an extra egg for the pan.)
> Water (And you need a tablespoon of water for each egg.)
> Salt
> Pepper (There's something important you should know about pepper. That's this: The ground pepper you buy in a box at the grocery store is okay, *but if your mother has a pepper mill* and you can grind whole peppercorns yourself, it tastes a whole lot pepperier. So I always say, *"Grind it yourself!"*)
> Butter or margarine (You need a tablespoon for each egg. Ask your mother or father to show you how to measure butter.)

1. Break the eggs into a bowl. (IF YOU'VE NEVER BROKEN AN EGG BEFORE, ASK YOUR MOTHER OR FATHER TO BREAK THE FIRST ONE AND SHOW YOU HOW IT'S DONE.)

2. Measure the water into the bowl with the eggs. Put in a little salt and pepper. I can't tell you how much, because I don't know how many people you're cooking

for. A quick small shake of salt and one grind of pepper for each person might be about right.

3. Now beat it all together with a fork or a wire whisk or an egg beater. You don't need to make a big deal out of it. Just be sure the eggs are all mixed up and friendly.

4. Get out the big black frying pan. IMPORTANT NOTE: IF YOUR MOTHER USES TEFLON FRYING PANS, YOU SHOULD ONLY USE ONE TABLE-SPOON OF BUTTER (OR MAYBE TWO) NO MAT-TER HOW MANY EGGS YOU'RE SCRAMBLING. THE REASON IS THAT THINGS DON'T STICK TO TEFLON, BUT YOU STILL NEED A LITTLE BUT-TER FOR FLAVOR. So put the butter in the frying pan and turn the heat to low.

5. When the butter is melted—it shouldn't be bubbling —pour the eggs into the frying pan. Leave them alone for about 30 seconds. And then you have to get to work.

6. Take a wooden spoon or a spatula and start stirring them around. Keep pushing the part that starts to get firm around the edge of the pan into the middle. It gets to be like a game.

7. When the eggs seem to be pretty well set and not runny, turn off the heat. But keep stirring the eggs for about another 30 seconds, because the heat of the pan keeps cooking them, even though you turned the heat off.

8. Now it's time to serve. If you fried some bacon and have it waiting in the oven, dish out the scrambled eggs into the middle of a platter and arrange the bacon strips around the eggs so they will look good.

GOOD IDEAS: After you've scrambled eggs on your own a couple of times, you may want to try something different. For instance, you can cut up little pieces of ham or some cheese and scramble them with the eggs. Or crumble up a piece of cooked bacon and use that. If you like onion flavor, cut up (BE CAREFUL WITH THE KNIFE. UNLESS YOU ARE FAIRLY EXPERIENCED, REMEMBER THAT WE HAVE A RULE—PARENTS HAVE TO STAND BY WHILE JUNIOR COOKS USE SHARP KNIVES AND MACHINES LIKE ELECTRIC MIXERS AND BLENDERS. OKAY?) Anyway, cut up the green part of scallions or some chives and mix them in.

I know a boy who scrambled some popped corn with his eggs. But he only did that once.

PARLEZ-VOUS FRENCH TOAST?

Well, you don't have to speak French to cook French toast—or to eat it. French toast is a very special Sunday breakfast. (We have it for supper, too, once in a while.) Here's how you make it. You'll need:

     2 eggs
     ½ teaspoon of salt
     ¾ cup of milk
     6 slices of bread
        Butter
        Maple syrup (Or apple sauce or confection-
           ers' sugar or sugar and cinnamon mixed
           together or almost anything you like. Some
           people like chocolate syrup.)

1. Put your apron on and break the eggs into a shallow bowl, or into a glass pie plate. ASK YOUR MOTHER WHAT TO USE. Beat the eggs with a fork or an egg

beater just a little, then add the salt and milk and beat just enough to mix everything up.

2. Cut each slice of bread in half and put 2 or 3 pieces into the milk and egg mixture. After about a minute, turn them over so the other side can soak up the egg mixture. You can use your fingers if you want, but be sure to wash your hands first.

3. Put about 2 tablespoons of butter into a big frying pan and turn on the heat. Ask your mother to show you how high.

4. When the frying pan is hot and the melted butter spreads all over the bottom of the pan, take the bread out of the bowl and put it in the frying pan. Put some more bread to soak in the milk and egg.

5. After a couple of minutes, turn the bread in the frying pan over with a spatula. It should be nice and toasty colored. And in a couple of more minutes, take it out of the frying pan.

6. Keep on until you've finished all the bread. When you finish cooking each piece of French toast, put it on a piece of aluminum foil in the oven. Turn the oven on to 300 degrees. This will keep your French toast warm until all the slices are cooked.

7. Now here's the fun—decide how you want to eat them. You can try any of the things suggested at the top. Maple syrup is very good, but you use what you like best.

PANCAKES
PLAIN AND FANCY

Pancakes for breakfast are as American as *Yankee Doodle Dandy*. And there are more ways to cook pancakes than there are states in these United States. I'll tell you about a few different ways to make them here, and you may be able to invent your own pancake variation once you've gotten the hang of making pancakes.

BASIC FLAPJACKS

I suppose it's sort of silly to give you a recipe for pancakes (Flapjacks is another name for them. It's a little old-fashioned, but don't you like the way it sounds? FLAPJACKS!) because all the boxes of pancake flour have directions on them, but I think mine are easier to understand.

You need:

> 1 cup pancake mixture (Almost any kind is good. Buckwheat, I think, is *very* good.)
> 1 egg
> 1 tablespoon of salad oil—like corn oil or safflower oil
> 1 cup milk
> Butter
> Maple syrup

1. First of all, wash your hands. It may not make the pancakes taste any better, but they'll certainly be less germy. Put everything except the butter and the maple syrup into a bowl and stir it all around 10 times. Don't

worry if there are lumps and bumps. Ten good stirs is enough.

2. Put 1 tablespoon of butter in a big frying pan and turn the heat on so it gets hot and the butter bubbles and goes all over the pan.

3. Now, take a small measuring cup—the ¼-cup size. Fill it with the pancake mixture and pour it into the frying pan. You should have room for three pancakes. When the pancake starts to have bubbles break through the top, turn it over and let it get brown on the other side. If you're not sure that it's brown, just lift it up with the spatula and peek. It won't hurt the pancake.

4. Sometimes the first pancake just doesn't look right. But it usually tastes all right. So don't worry.

5. Call everybody to breakfast and keep making pancakes until the batter is all used up. Serve the pancakes with maple syrup and butter. That's the way to start the day.

IF YOU WANT TO SHOW OFF: And why not? You can make your own pancake mixture and not bother with buying the packaged stuff at the store. It's easier than you think.

All you need is:

> 1 cup of flour
> 1 teaspoon of salt
> 3 tablespoons of sugar
> 1 tablespoon of baking powder

1. Measure everything into a flour sifter.

2. Sift everything into a mixing bowl. And there you have it—your own pancake mixture. Now, isn't that easy? It's cheaper, too.

GOOD IDEA ONE: You can make your own pancake

mixture ahead of time and keep it in an old coffee can or a glass jar with a screw-on top. Paste a label on the container. For instance, Mabel McAllister's Private Pancake Mixture.

GOOD IDEA TWO: You can experiment a little. For instance, use buckwheat flour instead of white flour. Or use ¾ cup of white flour and ¼ cup of wheat germ. Perhaps you'll invent a completely original and delicious pancake.

GOOD IDEA THREE: This makes a good present. You could make three or four cups of your own pancake mixture and put it in an old coffee can that you have painted and decorated yourself. This is a great Christmas present or hostess present to take along when you go visit someone for the weekend. People like it especially because you did it yourself.

FRUITY FLAPJACKS

There are umpty-ump different kinds of fruity flapjacks. Here's a chance to learn how to be a creative cook and find out what flavors go together best.

Make the basic flapjack mixture and add:

 ¾ cup of blueberries
   or
 1 apple (Peel it first, of course, and slice it thin.
   PLEASE BE CAREFUL WITH THAT
   KNIFE.)
   or
 1 medium bunch of seedless white grapes
   or
 ½ cup of cranberries
   or
 · 1 banana (Peel it and slice it.)

1. Add the fruits after you've given the pancake batter five stirs. Then give it five stirs more and it's ready to meet the heat.

GOOD IDEA: You might try throwing in a small handful of nuts, too, if you like. For instance, sliced strawberries and almond slivers are a good combination. So are sliced bananas and chopped walnuts. Can you think of other good combinations?

MEATY GRIDDLE CAKES

Someone said that these are the end of the trail for leftovers. Well, if there's a little bit of leftover ham in the refrigerator or you just happened to cook an extra strip of bacon (or two), you certainly wouldn't want to waste them. Would you? Griddle cakes? That's just another word (or two) for pancakes or flapjacks.

Here's the kind of thing to use (incidentally, it's important to use your imagination, too):

> 1 or 2 slices of leftover ham or chicken
> or
> 1 or 2 slices of cooked bacon
> or
> 1 or 2 or 3 cooked breakfast sausages
> or
> Chipped beef (about half a handful)
> Etcetera (Do you know what that means?
> ASK YOUR MOTHER OR FATHER IF
> YOU DON'T.)

1. Now, depending on what you have, cut it up or tear it up into small pieces—oh, about the size of your little fingernail.

2. Prepare the Basic Flapjack Mixture and add your small pieces of meat after you've given the batter the first five stirs. Then stir it five more times to mix the meat in evenly and you're ready to have them meet the griddle.

WARNING: FOR HEAVEN'S SAKE, PLEASE MAKE SURE THAT THE LEFTOVERS YOU PUT IN YOUR MEATY GRIDDLE CAKES AREN'T SOMETHING YOUR MOTHER WAS SAVING FOR LUNCH. ASK FIRST—OR WE'LL BOTH BE IN TROUBLE.

FLYING SAUCER PANCAKE

This is just about the biggest pancake I've ever met. Read the recipe all the way through and then get together:

> 2 eggs
> ½ cup of flour
> ½ cup of milk
> 4 tablespoons of butter (Just remember there are 8 tablespoons in each quarter-pound stick of butter. So if you cut a stick in half, you'll have—how much? That's right. Exactly 4 tablespoons.)
> 2 tablespoons of confectioners' sugar or regular white sugar
> ½ lemon

1. Turn the oven on to 425 degrees. And wash your hands. And put on a clean apron. (YOU KNOW WHAT ONE OF THE WORLD'S BEST APRONS IS? ONE OF YOUR FATHER'S OLD SHIRTS. JUST CUT OFF THE SLEEVES. BUT, PLEASE, MAKE SURE IT'S AN OLD SHIRT BEFORE YOU CUT OFF THE SLEEVES.)

2. Break the 2 eggs into a mixing bowl. If you started cooking from the beginning of this chapter, you should be very good at breaking eggs by now. If you didn't, ASK YOUR MOTHER TO SHOW YOU HOW TO BREAK THEM PROPERLY. Beat the eggs with the egg beater or a fork or a wire whisk just enough to get the yolks and the whites mixed up.

3. Add the flour and the milk and beat a little more. The mixture should *NOT* be smooth, so don't beat too much.

4. Now get out the biggest black frying pan in the cupboard or perhaps YOUR MOTHER HAS A VERY LARGE SHALLOW OVENPROOF DISH. This flying saucer pancake fits best in a 12-inch skillet. If you don't have anything that big, you can use two smaller pans. ASK YOUR MOTHER'S ADVICE. AND BE SURE THAT THE PANS DON'T HAVE WOODEN HAN-DLES, BECAUSE THEY'LL BE GOING IN THAT HOT 425-DEGREE OVEN.

5. Put the butter in the frying pan. When it's all melted and just bubbling, pour in the batter. Then put the whole thing in the oven.

6. The Flying Saucer takes 15 to 20 minutes to cook. It's done when it is a golden brown color. Take it out then and sprinkle the sugar all over the top. Then put it back in the oven for just 1 minute. BE CAREFUL. IT'S HOT, HOT, HOT!

7. Use that 1 minute to squeeze the half lemon.

8. Take the Flying Saucer out of the oven. Sprinkle the lemon juice over the top. It's ready to eat. (I forgot to mention one thing. You're not supposed to eat the whole pancake yourself. It's enough for four hungry people. So cut it up like a pie—in wedges.

GOOD IDEA: You could serve this with a little currant jelly or strawberry jam or cut-up fresh strawberries for a Sunday brunch. It's very impressive.

BEN'S EATEMALLUP MUFFINS

I don't know who invented the muffin, but Ben—he's twelve now—is a muffin master. He makes muffins almost every Sunday morning. And he started when he was eight. This is the recipe he uses. Ben says it's as easy as pie. (I think it's easier than pie.)

Ben uses:

- 2 cups of flour
- 3 teaspoons of baking powder
- 1 teaspoon of salt
- ¼ cup of sugar
- 1 large egg or 2 small ones
- 1 cup of milk
- ¼ cup of corn oil or melted butter

1. If you haven't made it a habit yet, please go wash your hands and put on your apron. Then turn the oven on to 400 degrees.

2. Get out the muffin tins (This recipe makes 12 muffins.) and butter them carefully. Some people use paper muffin cups to save the bother of buttering, but I think that this is an unnecessary use of paper and just wastes our natural resources. You know they have to cut down trees to make paper. So, butter your muffin tins and then wash your hands again.

3. Now, measure all the dry things—the flour, the baking powder, the salt and the sugar—into the flour sifter and then sift it all into a mixing bowl.

4. Then put all the wet things into another bowl. Break the egg (YOU LEARNED HOW TO DO THAT WHEN YOU MADE FRIENDLY EGGS) into the bowl and add the milk and oil. Beat it with an egg beater until everything is mixed up well.

5. Now pour the contents of the wet bowl into the dry bowl and stir it around. Don't stir very much. Be a little lazy. You just want to get the wet and dry ingredients mixed together.

6. Now you're ready. Spoon your muffin batter into the buttered muffin tins. Fill each cup just a smidgen more than halfway up.

7. Put them in the oven and bake them for 15 minutes. While they're baking, you might just as well wash your cooking dishes and get them out of the way.

8. Take the muffins out of the oven. BE CAREFUL. USE TWO POT HOLDERS. YOU CERTAINLY DON'T WANT TO BURN YOUR FINGERS. Turn the muffin pans upside down on a wire rack.

9. The muffins should just slip out. But sometimes they don't do what they should. When that happens, slide a spatula or a knife around the edge to loosen the muffin. BE CAREFUL. THE PANS ARE PROBABLY STILL HOT.

10. It's time to eat. If there are any muffins left over, you can split them and toast them for breakfast the next morning.

MUFFIN TRICKS: If you're having bacon for breakfast, cook two extra strips. Crumble them up and add them to the dry ingredients after they've been sifted into the bowl. Or you could add a handful of raisins. Or a couple of handfuls of blueberries. (If you use blueberries, add 2 or 3 more tablespoons of sugar.)

MUFFINS-IN-DISGUISE

Here's another trick with muffins. No one suspects that it's just plain old Eatemallup Muffins.

Here's what you do:

1. Heat the oven to 375 degrees. Then butter an 8-inch-square pan. If you don't have one, a 9-inch-square pan is all right.

2. Make the muffin batter and pour it in the pan.

3. Sprinkle the top with cinnamon sugar. That's easy to make. You just mix 1 teaspoon of cinnamon with ½ cup of sugar.

4. Bake your Muffins-In-Disguise for 25 minutes.

5. After 25 minutes, take the pan out of the oven. Place it on a wire rack and let it cool for about 5 minutes. Then cut it in squares right in the pan. Lift the squares out with a spatula and serve them warm.

EXTRA: You can add blueberries if you like, but don't forget the extra sugar.

CORNFLAKE CAKE (YES, CORNFLAKE CAKE!)

Cereal can get pretty boring morning after morning after morning. Here's a way to have your cereal and like it a lot.

You need:

> 4 tablespoons of butter (Remember how you measured the butter for the Flying Saucer Pancake? If there are 8 tablespoons of butter in a quarter-pound stick, how much do you need for 4 tablespoons? Half a stick, right?)
>
> 2½ cups of cornflakes
>
> 5 or 6 apples
>
> ½ lemon
>
> ½ cup of brown sugar (If your mother doesn't have brown sugar, white is okay. It's just not quite as delicious.)
>
> 1 teaspoon of cinnamon
>
> ½ cup of hot apple juice (If you don't have apple juice, you can use just plain hot water.)

1. Turn the oven on to 350 degrees.

2. Put the butter in a little saucepan and melt it over low heat. When it's melted, turn off the heat and stir in the cornflakes so they'll get buttery all over.

3. Now you have to get the apples ready. You'll need a sharp paring knife. ASK YOUR MOTHER TO HELP YOU WITH THIS. YOU DON'T WANT TO CUT YOURSELF—JUST THE APPLES. PERHAPS SHE CAN DO HALF THE APPLES TO SHOW YOU HOW, THEN YOU DO THE OTHER HALF WHILE SHE KEEPS AN EYE ON YOU. The apples have to be peeled, then cut in quarters. That makes it easier to cut out the core. Then they have to be sliced. Try to make the slices all the same size—as near as you can.

4. Squeeze the lemon and put the juice aside until you need it.

5. Grate the lemon rind. ASK YOUR MOTHER TO SHOW YOU HOW. AND BE CAREFUL. YOU DON'T

WANT TO GRATE THE SKIN OFF YOUR FINGERS. IT WON'T MAKE THE CAKE TASTE ANY BETTER.

6. The next step is to mix the brown sugar, cinnamon, and grated lemon rind together in a little bowl or cup.

7. Now you have to decide what you're going to bake your cake in. I use a white porcelain soufflé dish. But a glass casserole is just as good. For that matter, there's nothing wrong with a plain old cake pan; it just doesn't seem to show off the Cornflake Cake as much. Anyway, choose your pan or dish and butter it carefully.

8. This part is fun. Cover the bottom of your baking dish with a third of the buttered cornflakes (don't try to divide it down to the last cornflake, this is just a rough measure). Then make a neat layer of half the sliced apples on top of the cornflakes. Then sprinkle half the sugar, cinnamon and lemon-rind mixture over the apples.

9. Now put half the remaining buttered cornflakes over the whole thing. Make another layer with the rest of the apple slices and sprinkle the rest of the sugar, cinnamon and lemon rind over them. Then top the whole thing with the last of the cornflakes.

10. Pour the lemon juice over the top. Then pour the hot apple juice very slowly over the top and pop your Cornflake Cake into the oven.

11. Tear off a piece of aluminum foil and place it loosely over the top for the first 10 minutes so the cornflakes won't get too brown.

12. Bake the Cornflake Cake for 40 minutes. Then take it out of the oven and tell everyone that breakfast is ready.

GOOD IDEA ONE: For an extra-healthy dish, use a cup of toasted wheat germ in place of one of the cups of cornflakes. Wheat germ has lots of Vitamin B_1 and B_2 to help you grow and have good skin and shiny hair. It's good for your teeth, too.

GOOD IDEA TWO: You can make this in the after-noon when you get home from school or in the evening if your homework is finished. Then all you have to do in the morning is warm it up in a 350-degree oven for 10 minutes.

GOOD IDEA THREE: This Cornflake Cake is so good, you can serve it for dessert as well as for breakfast. For a company dessert, just add a little vanilla ice cream or some whipped cream.

OATMEAL, YECCH!

Jeff used to say "Yecch!" whenever there was oatmeal for breakfast, but when he had this special oatmeal, he changed. Instead of saying "Oatmeal, Yecch!" Jeff began to say "Oatmeal, yum!" I bet you'll say the same thing if you try this recipe.

Here's what you need:

1 cup of steel-cut oatmeal (This is NOT the yicky kind of oatmeal that comes in those round boxes and says quick-cooking or something. This oatmeal is not flaky or powdery. It's just cut-up bits of real oats. It even tastes good when you nibble it before it's cooked. It costs more than the other, but tastes so-o-o much better.)

3 cups of boiling water

1 teaspoon of salt

½ cup of raisins

¼ cup of brown sugar

1 teaspoon of cinnamon

2 tablespoons of butter

1. Get out the double boiler. Fill the bottom part al-most halfway up with hot water. Put it on the stove and turn the heat up to medium.

2. Place the steel-cut oatmeal in the top of the double boiler. Then add the 3 cups of boiling water, and the teaspoon of salt. Then fit the top into the bottom of the double boiler.

3. Stir the oatmeal and water for 1 minute. Then put the cover on and let it cook. After 10 minutes stir it again for 1 minute. Let it cook for another 10 minutes. (It's fun to watch. It makes little pouting bubbles. Do you see them?)

4. Now, add the raisins, the sugar, the cinnamon and the butter and stir everything together. Put the cover on and let it all cook for just 5 minutes more.

5. It's ready. Dish it out into cereal bowls. If you want, sprinkle a little more brown sugar on top. Oatmeal, YUM!

OATBURGERS

If you have any leftover oatmeal, here's what to do with it. In our house we always make too much oatmeal, so we'll be sure to have some left over to make Oatburgers.

You'll need:

    2 cups of cold oatmeal (If you have any left-
        over Oatmeal, Yecch!, that's perfect.)
    1 egg
    1 tablespoon of water
    1 cup (about—maybe you'll need more) of wheat
        germ
    2 tablespoons of butter
        Maple syrup

1. Shape the cold oatmeal into little patties like hamburgers.

2. Break the egg in a small bowl, add the water and beat with a fork or wire whisk until it's just a little foamy.

3. Measure the wheat germ out on a big plate.

4. Now the fun begins. Roll an Oatburger around in the egg and water, then roll it around in the wheat germ. When it's nicely coated with the wheat germ, put it on a plate and then do the same thing with the rest of the Oatburgers.

5. When you've finished, put the butter in a big frying pan. When it's melted, put the Oatburgers in the frying pan and cook them for about 5 minutes on each side.

6. Serve them with maple syrup. Most people will want two, at least.

LAZY LUCY'S WAKE-UP RICE

Lucy wasn't really lazy. She just didn't like to get up in the morning. So she invented a breakfast that she could cook the night before. People usually don't think of having rice for breakfast, but why not. It's a cereal—and it's good for you. Lazy Lucy's Rice has fruit in it, too. That makes it extra good.

You need:

    ½ pound of dried apricots (You can use prunes
           if you don't have apricots.)
    ¼ cup of sugar (white or brown)
    1 cup of rice
  2½ cups of water
    1 teaspoon of salt
    1 tablespoon of butter
    1 teaspoon of cinnamon

1. Put the apricots in a pan and add enough water to cover them. Then put them on the stove and cook them slowly for half an hour. Keep an eye on them. You may have to add a little more water.

2. After half an hour, add the sugar and stir the apricots so it gets all mixed in. Let the apricots cook 5 more minutes.

3. While the apricots are cooking, measure the rice, the 2½ cups of water and the salt into another pan. Put it on the stove and when the water starts to boil, cover the pan and turn the heat down as low as it will go.

4. Let the rice cook over the low heat for 15 minutes.

5. When the apricots are done, take them off the heat and let them cool a little. When they're cool enough (Did you wash your hands?) so you can handle them without getting burned, cut them up into small pieces. Each apricot should make three or four pieces, depending on how big it is.

6. Now put the rice, the apricots and any liquid that was left in the apricot pan in the top of a double boiler. Add the butter and the cinnamon. Stir everything up and put the cover on the top of the double boiler.

7. Fill the bottom part of the double boiler almost halfway up with water. Fit the top part into it. And that's it. Just leave it on the stove until morning.

8. When Lazy Lucy gets up in the morning, she just turns on the heat under the double boiler. Breakfast is piping hot and ready to eat in 15 minutes.

9. Serve the rice in cereal bowls. Some people like it with milk. Others sprinkle a little more brown sugar over it. Some do both. And some people eat it just the way it is. How do you like it?

GOOD IDEA: This is so easy to make, you can cook it

while you're helping with the dishes after dinner. Or, if you have a timer on your stove, you could be doing your homework while you wait for the apricots and rice to cook.

GLOP ON TOAST

This is a perfectly horrible name for a perfectly delicious dish. The way this got started was one morning one of the boys said, "I'm starved. Why don't you make some of that glop on toast for breakfast?" So I did. And that's what we've called it ever since. Some people refer to it as chipped beef on toast.

You'll need:

¼ pound of chipped beef (It usually comes in 4-ounce jars. How many jars will you need? I'll give you a hint. There are 16 ounces in a pound.)

¼ cup of butter or margarine

2 cups of milk (Some people use 1 cup of milk and 1 of cream, but that makes it rather rich—and it's more expensive, too.)

¼ cup of flour

4 slices of bread

Black pepper (And I'll say it again: It's better if you grind it yourself.)

½ teaspoon of grated nutmeg (And this is better if you grate it yourself, but the kind that comes in the box is all right.)

1. Put the chipped beef in a colander and pour hot water over it. If the water from your hot-water faucet is really hot, that's fine. If not, boil some and pour it over.

This is to get the extra-salty taste out of the chipped beef. As soon as the beef is cool enough to touch, pull it apart with your fingers (You *did* wash your hands, didn't you? That's good.) and tear the larger pieces into small ones.

2. Now you're going to make a cream sauce. When you learn how to do this, you've learned a very important step in cooking. A cream sauce is the basis of a lot of good eating.

Here's What You Do:

3. Melt the butter in the top of the double boiler. Remember to put water in the bottom part—a little less than half full—before you place the top part into it.

4. While the butter is melting, put the 2 cups of milk in a pan and heat it over low heat. When the milk starts getting little bubbles around the edge, turn off the heat.

5. As soon as the butter is melted, stir in the flour with a wooden spoon or a wire whisk. It's important to keep stirring all the time so that the flour and butter get together smoothly.

6. This is the tricky part. (It's not really *that* tricky.) ASK YOUR MOTHER TO HELP YOU THE FIRST TIME. SHE MIGHT POUR WHILE YOU STIR. Pour the hot milk slowly into the flour and butter mixture. Don't stop stirring for a minute—even while you're pouring. (Wouldn't it be handy to have three hands? Too handy, I guess.) If you stop stirring, your sauce will get lumpy. It should be nice and smooth. Keep on stirring after all the milk has been added and pretty soon you will notice that the sauce is starting to get thick. When it starts to get thick, keep stirring for 3 more minutes. Then add the chipped beef.

7. Stir it just enough to mix the beef in the sauce. Then

leave it on low heat while you make toast. Cut each piece of toast into triangles. It looks better that way. Or you can split and toast English muffins. They're very good.

8. Use a ladle or a small measuring cup to pour the chipped beef over the toast or muffins. Grind just a little pepper on top. And sprinkle the nutmeg—just a tiny bit—over each serving.

GOOD IDEAS: Now that you know how to make chipped beef, here are ways you can vary it. You can use ham instead of chipped beef. Cut it up in little cubes. You can slice up the green part of scallions (you'll need about a quarter of a cup) and add them to the sauce along with the chipped beef or ham. Perhaps you can think of other ways to transform this recipe. For instance, what about chicken?

TWO

A BAKER'S DOZEN
of
LUNCHTIME
SPECIALS

In today's busy world, no one wants to spend a lot of time cooking lunch. Busy mothers just perch on a stool at the kitchen counter and have a quick snack. A lot of fathers just have a sandwich at their desks. And most people between the ages of seven and seventeen take their lunches to school.

On weekends, things are a little different. Saturdays are a good time for parents—and that means fathers, you know, as well as mothers—and children to cook together. And they're a great time to invite friends over to sample your cooking at lunch.

In this chapter, there's a little something for every luncher—quick snacks, company lunches, weekend lunches—even some good suggestions for the dieter's school lunch box. (Did you ever try a mustard sandwich? Yummy! Honest!)

MACARONI AND YOU-KNOW-WHAT

The mystery ingredient is cheese, of course. This is great for lunch or supper. If you want, you can bake it in three or four small aluminum foil pans and eat one now and freeze the others. Then some day when you're in a real hurry, you can just pop one in the oven and bake it at 400 degrees for 20 or 30 minutes (It's done when it gets bubbly on top.). You'll find that your macaroni and cheese casserole tastes a lot better than the frozen ones you buy at the store. You know why? That's right—because you use better ingredients and no chemical preservatives. It's just bound to be better.

Now, remember, always read the recipe all the way through before you start. And always wash your hands before you start.

Put your apron on and get together:

1 8- or 9-ounce package of elbow macaroni
2 cups of grated Cheddar cheese (Please buy it in a hunk. Get the kind they call "rat cheese" and grate it yourself. WATCH YOUR FINGERS WHILE YOU'RE GRATING.)
2 cups of cream sauce (This is the same cream sauce you made for Glop on Toast. The recipe is on page 48.)
(Here's what you can add next time to make your macaroni and cheese different. You can cut 2 frankfurters into half-inch pieces and add them. Or you can put in little bits of leftover ham or chicken. You can cut up a couple of tomatoes and mix them in. Just use your imagination and think what might go well together. You're the cook. BUT

PLEASE DON'T USE UP ANYTHING YOUR MOTHER IS SAVING. ASK FIRST.)

1. Turn on the oven to 375 degrees.

2. Make 2 cups of the cream sauce.

3. Cook the macaroni just the way it tells you on the package, EXCEPT—and this is important—COOK IT ONE MINUTE LESS THAN IT SAYS. The reason is that it's going to cook more later. BE SURE TO ASK YOUR MOTHER FOR HELP WHEN IT'S TIME TO DRAIN THE MACARONI. YOU DON'T WANT TO GET BURNED.

4. Now take that big hunk of cheese and grate it. PLEASE ASK YOUR MOTHER TO SHOW YOU HOW TO DO IT PROPERLY. I DON'T WANT YOU TO GRATE YOUR KNUCKLES. JUST THE CHEESE.

5. Everything should be all set now. Get a 1½-quart baking dish and grease the bottom and sides with a little butter or margarine. Now spread half the macaroni over the bottom.

6. Then cover the macaroni with three quarters of a cup of the grated cheese.

7. Cover the grated cheese with another layer of the macaroni. Use it all up. And then make another layer of three quarters of a cup of cheese.

8. Pour the 2 cups of cream sauce over the top. Try to distribute it evenly.

9. Now, how much cheese do you have left? That's right. Half a cup. Sprinkle it over the top of the casserole. It's ready to go in the oven.

10. Bake your macaroni and cheese casserole until the cheese on top gets all bubbly and turns a golden brown color.

FIRST NOTE: If you plan to freeze part of your casserole, you just get out three or four small aluminum foil pans and fill them up just the way I told you to fill the big casserole. Be careful about dividing things up evenly.

SECOND NOTE: If you are adding anything extra like tomatoes or little bits of ham, the time to put them in is after the first layer of cheese.

BLT ON TOAST

Do you know what this is? BLT is what the waitress at the lunch counter calls a bacon, lettuce and tomato sandwich. It saves time. And you'll save time if you read the recipe through first.

Get together:

> 2 or 3 pieces of bacon
> 2 slices of white or whole wheat bread
> Mayonnaise
> 2 leaves of lettuce (Use Boston lettuce, not iceberg.)
> 2 slices of a ripe red tomato
> This is enough for one sandwich. If you're getting lunch for more people, you just multiply everything by the number of people. Now, if you've done your arithmetic—

1. Wash your hands and fry the bacon. (Turn back to the Breakfast chapter and follow the directions for Alarm Clock Bacon. It's on page 27.)

2. Toast the bread. Spread one side of each slice with mayonnaise. Then put a lettuce leaf on top of the mayonnaise on one piece of toast.

3. Arrange the tomato slices and bacon on the lettuce leaf. If you break the bacon in half, it will fit better.

4. Some people add a little more mayonnaise at this point. It depends on how much you like mayonnaise. You do whatever you like.

5. Now cover the bacon and tomato with the other lettuce leaf and top it off with the other piece of toast (mayonnaise side down, please).

6. That's it. Drink a glass of milk with your BLT and you'll be chock-block full of vitamins and proteins and minerals. It's good with lemonade, too.

PHONY PIZZA

Real pizza takes a lot of time—and muscle—to make. But this pizza is a real quickie. Some kids like it as an after-school snack. It's a good lunch with a salad or some carrot sticks or coleslaw.

You need:

    4 English muffins
    4 tablespoons of butter or margarine
    4 tablespoons of ketchup
  16 slices of salami
    4 slices of processed American cheese (Or you can use mozzarella or Muenster. Suit yourself.)
    1 teaspoon of dried oregano (If your MOTHER doesn't have this on her herb and spice shelf, ask her to get it. You can use it a lot in cooking.)

And now to work:

1. Split the muffins in half. They taste better if you use a fork to split them instead of cutting them with a knife. I don't know why, but they just do. ASK YOUR MOTHER TO SHOW YOU HOW TO SPLIT THEM WITH A FORK.

2. Butter the muffins and put them under the broiler until they are toasty brown. ASK YOUR MOTHER OR FATHER TO TURN ON THE BROILER AND STICK AROUND WHILE YOU TOAST THE MUFFINS.

3. Now spread a little ketchup on each muffin. Put 2 slices of salami on each one and top it with half a slice of cheese. Sprinkle a little oregano over the cheese.

4. Put them back under the broiler until the cheese is melted and bubbly.

5. Let them cool just a little bit before you start eating. You don't want to burn your tongue. This is enough for four girls or two boys.

KEN'S DOUBLE FEATURE

Some people can't decide whether they like hamburgers or hot dogs better. Ken solved the problem by inventing the Double Feature. It's his favorite Saturday lunch.

Here's what he uses:

    1 hot dog
    1 pound of ground beef, chuck or round
        Butter or margarine
    4 hamburger rolls
    2 tablespoons of ketchup (You might like more.
        It's a free country. Suit yourself.)
    2 tablespoons of green relish (Maybe you'll like
        more of this, too.)

4 slices of onion (Some people just love raw onion. Other people *hate* it. Use your judgment. If you decide you want onion, PLEASE BE VERY CAREFUL WITH THAT KNIFE WHEN YOU SLICE IT.)

1. Cut the hot dog into four equal pieces.

2. Wash your hands, will you? Now divide the ground beef into four parts and shape it into patties. The secret is to shape the hamburger around a piece of hot dog so that no one can tell that it's inside. Okay?

3. Now get out that big black frying pan. Put a smidgen (that's a very small piece) of butter in it and turn on the heat. IF YOU HAVEN'T COOKED MUCH, ASK YOUR MOTHER TO REGULATE THE HEAT FOR YOU. The hamburgers should cook about 4 minutes on each side. It depends on how well done you like them.

4. While they're cooking, split the rolls and put them in the oven to warm. The oven should be set at about 300 degrees.

5. When the rolls are warm, butter them and put the ketchup and relish on four of the halves.

6. Put a hamburger on top of the ketchup and relish. Add a little more ketchup and relish if you feel like it. And put a slice of onion on. Then cover it all up with the other half of the roll.

7. Ken usually eats two of these, but not everybody has such a big appetite. One might be just enough for you.

CANNY CASSEROLE

I know you don't want to be the kind of cook who just opens a can and thaws out some frozen package and calls it a meal. There's not much fun in that (and not much taste either). But once in a while, there just isn't time to cook things from scratch. Here's a casserole you can almost *throw* together. All you need to do is open some cans. But be careful when you're opening them.

You'll need:

> 1 can of cream of mushroom soup or cream of
>   celery soup
> ½ cup of milk
> 1 can of tuna fish (the 8-ounce size)
> 1 can of peas (The little ones are best. Get the
>   8-ounce size.)
> 1 can of water chestnuts (You don't really
>   need this, but the water chestnuts add a
>   nice crunchy surprise.)
> 2 tablespoons of canned pimientos
>   Potato chips or corn chips
>   Actually, it's a good idea to keep these in-
>   gredients on the emergency shelf. You
>   never know when you'll have to whip up a
>   meal in a hurry.

1. Turn the oven on to 375 degrees.

2. Open all the cans. ASK YOUR MOTHER TO SHOW YOU HOW TO OPERATE THE CAN OPENER IF YOU'RE A BEGINNING COOK.

3. Pour the soup and milk into a 1½-quart casserole and mix them up.

4. Then dump in the tuna fish, the peas and the water chestnuts. If the water chestnuts didn't come sliced, you can slice them.

5. Add the pimientos and stir the whole thing up with gusto. (That means with enthusiasm and energy.) Sprinkle the potato chips over the top and put the casserole in the oven.

6. This takes about 25 minutes to cook.

7. While it's cooking, you can make a green salad. (The Beginner's Basic Salad Kit is on page 88.) Wasn't that really easy? And there's only one cooking dish to wash!

BASIC CHICKEN SOUP

Now we're getting into real cooking. Chicken is the cook's best friend, because there are more than five hundred ways to serve it. That's right, five hundred. And once you learn to make this basic chicken soup, you're on your way to learning them. This takes time, so I suggest you plan to make it on a Saturday.

You'll need:

> 1 fowl, about 5 pounds. (A fowl is what they
> call a grown-up chicken.)
> 1 onion
> 4 cloves
> 1 carrot
> 2 sprigs of parsley
> 1 stalk of celery with the leaves on
> 12 peppercorns
> Salt
> Water
> ½ cup of rice (optional)
> 1 tablespoon of lemon juice

1. Wash the chicken off under cold running water. It may have a little package inside with gizzards and neck and liver. ASK YOUR MOTHER TO TELL YOU WHICH IS WHICH. If it does, put the gizzards and neck into a large kettle along with the chicken. SAVE THE CHICKEN LIVER. YOU CAN FRY IT IN A LIT-

TLE BIT OF BUTTER AND EAT IT ON TOAST. AND IT'S VERY GOOD WITH SCRAMBLED EGGS. YOU MAY WANT TO FRY IT AND CUT IT UP IN PIECES TO PUT IN SCRAMBLED EGGS (The recipe is on page 29.) FOR SUNDAY BREAKFAST.

2. Peel the onion. ASK YOUR MOTHER OR FATHER TO SUPERVISE IF YOU'RE A BEGINNING COOK. Now stick the cloves into the onion and put it in the big kettle.

3. Cut the top and bottom off the carrot and scrape it with a swivel-blade scraper. Add the carrot, the parsley, the celery and the 12 peppercorns to the kettle. And add some salt. I suggest you add about 2 teaspoons of salt now. You can add more later if you think it needs it. But always remember: IT'S EASY TO ADD MORE SALT, BUT IT'S VERY HARD TO DO MUCH ABOUT IT IF YOU PUT IN TOO MUCH.

4. Fill the kettle with cold water so that it comes just above the chicken and the other ingredients. About half an inch above is good.

5. Put the kettle on the stove. Turn on the heat and wait for the water to boil.

6. When the water boils, turn the heat down so that it will just simmer. It's simmering when there are little bubbles around the edge. ASK YOUR MOTHER TO TELL YOU WHEN IT'S SIMMERING IF YOU AREN'T SURE. Then put the cover on the kettle and let it simmer for 2 hours. You could clean your room, perhaps, while you're waiting.

7. All right, 2 hours are up. Take the chicken out of the kettle (ASK YOUR FATHER OR MOTHER TO HELP YOU) and put it on a platter or in a large bowl. As soon as it is cool enough for you to touch—for heaven's

sake, wash your hands first—pull the meat off the bones. Try to get as large pieces as you can. Wrap the chicken meat in plastic wrap or aluminum foil and put it in the refrigerator.

8. Put all the bones back in the kettle and simmer the soup for 45 minutes. Then pour it through a strainer into a big bowl or pan. ASK FOR HELP. THAT CHICKEN SOUP IS SCALDING HOT.

9. As soon as the broth has cooled a little, put it in the refrigerator for about an hour. The fat will rise to the top and you can skim it off. You don't need to get all the fat off, just most of it. ASK YOUR MOTHER WHAT TO DO WITH THE CHICKEN FAT. SOME PEOPLE LIKE TO USE IT FOR COOKING.

10. Courage. You're almost done. Heat the soup up again. Let it boil hard for about 5 minutes. Then taste it. Take a spoonful of soup and LET IT COOL BEFORE TASTING. If you think it needs more salt, this is the time to add it.

11. Take about a cup of the chicken meat, tear it into smallish pieces with your fingers and add it to the soup. If you like rice in your chicken soup, add half a cup right now. Simmer for 15 minutes.

12. Did you think I'd forgotten the lemon juice? This is the time to add it. Stir it in well.

13. Soup's served. If there's any left over, take good care of it. You can use it instead of milk to make the cream sauce for Macaroni and You-Know-What. And there are dozens of other uses for it in cooking. But I bet you won't have much left over. Isn't this a lot better than any chicken soup you ever warmed up from a can?

NOTE: You should have quite a bit of chicken left over. And that will be a beginning on more chicken rec-

ipes like Sally's Prize-Winning Chicken Salad, which is the
next recipe, and Tomato Hideaway (that's on page 64)
and Pete's Towers of Pisa (you'll find that on page 101).

SALLY'S PRIZE-WINNING CHICKEN SALAD

Sally entered this chicken salad at a county fair in
Maine the summer she was eleven—and she won a blue
ribbon. Your family will think you're a prize winner, too,
if you make Sally's salad for a special lunch—or maybe a
Sunday night supper.

Sally used:

> 1 head of Boston lettuce
> 1 bunch of watercress
> 4 sprigs of parsley
> 2 scallions
> 2 cups of cooked chicken cut up in little cubes
> (Use the chicken you have left over from
> making Basic Chicken Soup. Or you could
> use leftover roast chicken—except that
> there's hardly ever any leftover roast
> chicken.)
> 1 cup of chopped celery
> ½ cup of almonds (Once I used peanuts when
> I didn't have almonds. You could use
> water chestnuts. Or you could mix chunks
> of raw apple with walnuts. The main
> thing is to have something crunchy.)
> Mayonnaise, about 1 cup. You may want a
> little more or a little less.
> 2 tomatoes
> 2 hard-boiled eggs (We call them hard boiled,
> but you really shouldn't let them boil.
> Eggs should be cooked in water that is just
> simmering for about 25 minutes.)

Salt and pepper (Remember, pepper freshly ground from your pepper mill has a lot more taste.)

1. Wash your hands and then wash the lettuce and the watercress carefully. Tear off the toughest stems of the watercress and throw them away. Shake the greens in a salad basket to dry them, then wrap them in a clean dish towel and put them in the refrigerator while you prepare the rest of the salad.

2. Wash the parsley and chop it up finely. WATCH YOUR FINGERS. And while you have the chopping board out, cut the green part of the scallions into small pieces. This is a good time to chop the celery and cut up the chicken. Try to make the chicken cubes about the same size. It won't affect the taste, but it makes the salad look better.

3. Now put the parsley and scallions and chicken and celery in a large bowl.

4. Add the almonds to the bowl. You can use whole almonds or slivered ones. It doesn't really matter. I think they taste better when they're toasted. Here's what you do: turn the oven on to 400 degrees. Spread the almonds out on a cooky sheet and pop them in the 400-degree oven for about 3 minutes. Keep an eye on them so they won't burn.

5. Now add the mayonnaise and mix everything together very gently. It's a good idea to use two large spoons to do this. YOUR MOTHER CAN SHOW YOU HOW.

6. This is a good part: Taste the salad. Add a little salt and pepper. Easy on the salt. Remember it's better to add too little than too much. Now taste it again. More salt? It's up to you. You're the cook.

7. Shell the eggs and cut them in quarters the long way.

8. Wash the tomatoes and cut them in quarters, too. Cut off the little black stem ends.

9. All that's left to do is arrange the salad on the greens. Get out a large platter or a salad bowl. ASK YOUR MOTHER TO SUGGEST WHAT SHE THINKS WILL LOOK BEST. Arrange a base of lettuce leaves. Pile the salad in the middle of the leaves. Then arrange the eggs and tomatoes around the salad. Then add the watercress. You can place it around the eggs and tomatoes and put a few sprigs on top of the chicken mixture to decorate it. If you want, you can put extra mayonnaise on the platter or serve it separately.

TOMATO HIDEAWAY

Some people call this Tomato Surprise, because you don't know what's hidden away in the tomato until you start eating it. This is good to serve when you have friends over for lunch. It doesn't take much time to prepare and everybody likes it.

You'll need:

> 1 head of Boston lettuce
> 4 large, ripe, red tomatoes
> 2 cups of cooked chicken cut in little cubes
>   (You see, this is another way of serving the chicken that you cooked when you made Basic Chicken Soup.)
> 1 cup of chopped celery
> 1 cup of mayonnaise—more or less
> 1 bunch of parsley

1. Wash the lettuce in cold water, then put it in a salad basket and shake most of the water off. Wrap the lettuce in a clean dish towel and put it in the refrigerator while you get everything else ready.

2. Peel the tomatoes. You don't *really* need to do this, but it looks better. If you have a gas stove, hold the tomato over the flame with a fork and turn it until the skin splits. Then it's a cinch to slip the skin off. If you have an electric stove, drop the tomatoes one at a time into a pan of boiling water for about a minute. Then take them out and you'll find that the skin comes off fairly easily. MOTHERS: PLEASE KEEP AN EYE ON THIS GAS FLAME OR HOT-WATER OPERATION.

3. Now cut a slice off the top of the tomato and scoop out most of the insides with a spoon.

4. Mix the chicken and celery and mayonnaise together.

5. Taste it and see if it needs salt and pepper. If it does, just add a little at a time and keep tasting until it's just right. IMPORTANT WARNING: DON'T EAT TOO MUCH. JUST TASTE.

6. Now, very carefully, spoon the chicken salad into the four hollow tomatoes.

7. Wash the parsley. Dry it a little by squeezing it in a clean dish towel. Cut off the stems and then chop up the leafy bits with a sharp knife. CAREFUL. Sprinkle enough chopped parsley on the top of each tomato to completely hide the chicken salad.

8. Arrange two or three leaves of Boston lettuce as prettily as you can on each plate. Put a tomato in the center of the lettuce. And that's it.

NOTE: Potato chips are very good with this. And you might add some sliced sweet pickles if you like them.

HO HO, HO HO,
IT'S OFF TO SCHOOL WE GO!

If you take your lunch to school every day, it's apt to get pretty boring. Perhaps you are ready for a change. Here are two

LUNCH BOX SUPERSPECIALS
THE ENERGY SPECIAL

This is loaded with energy-makers. And it tastes good, too. There's another special thing about it: You can freeze it. So, if you follow this recipe, it will make four Energy Specials. You can take one to school today and freeze the rest. Then some morning when you're late, just grab an Energy Special out of the freezer. It will be thawed and ready to eat by lunchtime.

You need:

> 4 slices of bacon
> ½ cup of peanut butter (You can use more if
>   you want.)
> ¼ cup of apple sauce
> ¼ cup of wheat germ
> 1 apple
>   Butter
> 8 slices of whole wheat bread

1. Fry the bacon. Follow the Alarm Clock Bacon instructions on page 27.
2. Drain the cooked bacon on a couple of paper towels and crumble it in little bits.

3. Put the peanut butter, the apple sauce, the bacon and the wheat germ in a small bowl.

4. Wash the apple and grate it on the coarse side of the grater (ASK YOUR MOTHER TO HELP YOU) into the bowl with the peanut butter. You don't even have to pare the apple. Just be sure you don't grate the core—or your fingers.

5. Now butter the bread. Stir the mixture in the bowl until it's well mixed. Then spread it on four of the slices. Cover it with the other four slices.

6. If you want to freeze some of the sandwiches, ASK YOUR MOTHER TO SHOW YOU HOW TO WRAP THEM AND LABEL THEM FOR THE FREEZER.

GOOD IDEA: It's easier to make these the night before. Then you're not in such a rush and you have time to clean up and wash your dishes.

PEANUT-BUTTER-AND-JELLY WHAT?

Life isn't all peanut-butter-and-jelly sandwiches. There are peanut-butter-and-jelly waffles, for instance.

Here's what you need:

    2 frozen waffles
      Peanut butter
      Jelly (Use any kind you like. Or jam. You're
        the boss.)

Now do this:

1. Drop the waffles in the toaster and toast them.

2. Spread one waffle gently with peanut butter.

3. Spread the other gently with the jelly or jam of your choice.

4. Put the peanut butter and jelly sides together.
5. Cut the waffle sandwich in half.
6. Wrap. And pack in your lunch box.
7. Please don't eat it until lunchtime.

LINDA'S DIET LUNCHES

Linda was kind of pudgy when she was twelve, so she and her mother worked out some diet specials to pack in her school lunch box. They're high in protein and low in starches. If you are a little pudgy, too, you might want to try them. Here are three of Linda's diet specials.

MUSTARD (UH-HUH) SANDWICHES

Sound awful. They aren't. Just wait until you read how they're made. Your mother may even ask you to make them for hors d'oeuvres when she has a party. Do you know what hors d'oeuvres means? Well, you'd better look it up in the dictionary.

You'll need:

>   2 slices of boiled ham
>   Mustard
>   2 sprigs of parsley or watercress
>   2 stalks of celery
>   Toothpicks

Here's how you put it all together:
1. Spread one side of each slice of ham with mustard.
2. Then place a sprig of parsley or watercress and a

stalk of celery at one end of each slice of ham. Roll it up, so the ham is rolled around the celery and parsley and the mustard-side is inside.

3. Fasten each mustard sandwich with a toothpick. BUT PLEASE DON'T EAT THE TOOTHPICK, NO MATTER HOW HUNGRY YOU ARE.

KETCHUP (YUP) SANDWICHES

These were Linda's favorite. And I'll tell you a secret. I make them myself when I know I'm going to be busy and have to eat at my desk.

You'll need:

> 2 slices of roast beef
> Ketchup
> 2 sweet pickles
> Toothpicks

1. You make these just like you made the Mustard Sandwiches. Spread the ketchup on the roast beef.

2. Place the pickle at one end of the roast beef and roll the whole thing up—ketchup-side inside, of course.

3. Fasten the rolls with toothpicks or wrap them in aluminum foil to keep them together.

APPLE (WHY ARE YOU LAUGHING?) SANDWICHES

These are really delicious. And healthy, too. Here's how you make them. Take:

1 apple

4 slices of processed cheese (Use whatever you
like best—American or Swiss cheese are my
favorites.)

1. Wash the apple. Cut it in quarters. Then cut out the
core. REMEMBER—THE RULE IS THAT YOU ASK
YOUR MOTHER TO KEEP AN EYE ON YOU WHEN
YOU'RE USING SHARP KNIVES UNTIL YOU'VE
HAD PLENTY OF EXPERIENCE. OKAY?

2. Now cut the quarters into slices.

3. Spread the apple slices over two slices of the cheese.
Cover the apples with the other two slices.

4. Wrap the apple sandwiches securely in aluminum
foil so that apples won't slide out.

THREE

A BAKER'S DOZEN
of
THINGS TO COOK
FOR DINNER
(OR SUPPER)
AS THE CASE MAY BE

In many families, dinner time is the only time the whole family gets together. That makes the evening meal a very important event. It should be fun, too. Everyone should have a chance to talk and laugh and relax. This chapter tells you how to make some very thrifty meals—and some rather expensive ones. They're all family-tested. You'll learn how to make stews and pot roasts, salads and spaghetti with meatballs. And you'll be able to cook something different every night of the week—from an easy Saturday night supper to a company dinner.

By the time you and your mother (and your father, perhaps?) have cooked (and eaten) your way through this baker's dozen of recipes, you'll be a very competent cook. Just wait and see.

JEFF'S MESSY MACARONI

Jeff invented this version when he was eleven. Every family seems to have its own version.

Here's what you need:

½ pound of elbow macaroni
3 tablespoons of butter or margarine
2 onions
1 pound of ground beef, chuck or round
½ can of tomato paste, the 6-ounce size
2 cups of tomatoes (These can be canned or fresh. If they're fresh, cut them in quarters and cut off the stem end.)
Salt and pepper (Grind your own black pepper from your pepper mill. It's much better.)
LOTS of grated Parmesan cheese

1. Cook the macaroni just as it tells you on the package. When it's done, drain it. BE CAREFUL. ASK YOUR MOTHER TO HELP YOU SO YOU WON'T GET SCALDED BY THE BOILING WATER.

2. I'm sure you remembered to wash your hands, so go ahead and peel the onions. IF YOU'VE NEVER PEELED AN ONION BEFORE, ASK YOUR MOTHER TO SHOW YOU HOW TO DO THE FIRST ONE AND THEN SHE CAN WATCH YOU WHILE YOU DO THE SECOND ONION. Now, slice them up. You'll probably want to wash your hands again now—otherwise you'll smell like an onion the rest of the day.

3. Put the butter in a big frying pan. When it's melted, add the onion slices and cook at medium heat for 5 minutes. Stir the onions so they won't burn.

4. Add the ground beef to the onions. Now take a kitchen fork or a wooden spoon and push the meat around so it's all broken up. Keep stirring it until you can't see any more pink, and it's all cooked through. ASK YOUR MOTHER IF YOU AREN'T SURE IF IT'S COOKED ENOUGH.

5. Add a little salt and pepper and taste the meat and onions. Perhaps they need more salt? Okay, add a little more. Be careful. Don't add too much. Now add the tomato paste and the tomatoes.

6. Stir the whole thing around and keep on stirring and letting it bubble for 5 more minutes.

7. If the frying pan is really big, add the macaroni to the frying pan. If the frying pan is not big enough, put the macaroni and the meat mixture into a bigger pan. Stir it all around and let it cook slowly while you stir it until the macaroni is piping hot.

8. It's time to eat. Right now. Most people like to sprinkle their helpings with lots of grated Parmesan cheese.

BASIC SPAGHETTI

The simplest things are often the best. And this basic spaghetti is the proof. Make it for supper and serve it with a green salad and a loaf of crusty French or Italian

bread. Delicious. There won't be a single strand of spaghetti left over.

You'll need:

> 1 pound of spaghetti (This will make enough
>   for four people.)
> ¼ pound of butter
>   Salt and freshly ground pepper, please.
>   Plenty of grated Parmesan cheese (And re-
>   member, it really tastes a whole lot better
>   if you buy a chunk of Parmesan and grate
>   it yourself. Just don't grate your fingers.)

1. Cook the spaghetti just the way it tells you on the
package. It usually says "cook from 8 to 10 minutes." I
happen to think 8 minutes is better, because I like it just a
little chewy. The Italians call this *al dente*. But you suit
yourself. ASK YOUR MOTHER TO DRAIN THE SPA-
GHETTI FOR YOU. I DON'T WANT YOU TO GET
SCALDED FROM THAT HOT WATER.

2. As soon as the spaghetti is drained it should go in a
big bowl that has been warmed. (The best way is to run
hot water into the bowl and then wipe it dry just before
you put the spaghetti in.)

3. Now cut up the butter into four or five pieces and
put them in the spaghetti. Sprinkle a little salt and grind
some pepper over the spaghetti and then mix it up (use
two spoons, it's easier) until all the spaghetti is coated
with butter. If you need more butter, you can add a little,
but just a little.

4. Serve it. Isn't that simple? Just make sure there is
really plenty of grated cheese. Some people like extra
pepper, so put the pepper mill on the table, too.

SPAGHETTI AND MEATBALLS

This is a good company meal. It's a good family meal, too. Read the recipe all the way through and then tie on an apron and get together:

    1 pound of hamburger
    1 teaspoon of salt
    ½ teaspoon of pepper
    1 cup of chopped onion (Oh my! Are your eyes ever going to water! BE SURE YOUR MOTHER KEEPS AN EYE ON THE KNIFE WORK.)
    1 garlic clove
    ½ cup of olive oil (corn oil is okay, too.)
    2 cans of tomato paste, the 6-ounce size
    2½ cups of water
    1 tablespoon of chopped fresh basil (This is hard to get except in the summer. If you can't find it, use a teaspoon of dried basil or a teaspoon of dried thyme.)
    1 bay leaf
    1 pound of spaghetti
    Lots of grated Parmesan cheese (And will you please grate it yourself? The kind that comes already grated just doesn't have as much flavor.)

1. Wash your hands, please, and mix the hamburger with the salt and pepper and shape it into small meatballs. They should be about one inch in diameter.

2. Get a sharp knife (MOTHER, ARE YOU WATCHING?) and take the skin off the garlic clove, then chop the garlic into very small pieces. (THERE'S A TRICK THAT MAKES CHOPPING EASY AND FAST. YOU

LEAVE THE TIP OF YOUR KNIFE ON THE CHOP-PING BOARD AND THEN CHOP, CHOP, CHOP FROM LEFT TO RIGHT. ASK YOUR MOTHER TO SHOW YOU. THIS IS THE WAY PROFESSIONAL COOKS CHOP.

3. Now get out the big frying pan. Put the oil in it and put it on the stove. (MOTHER, YOU MIGHT KEEP AN EYE ON THIS.) Turn on the heat and when the oil is hot, add the chopped onion, the chopped garlic and the meatballs.

4. Turn the meatballs occasionally so they will get brown all over. Be careful, don't break them. When the onions are yellowish and sort of transparent, add the to-mato paste, the water, the basil and the bay leaf. Now simmer the whole thing over low heat for half an hour until it gets a little thick. Remember that simmering means that it's almost ready to boil, but not quite. Don't let it boil, keep watching it and adjust the heat if neces-sary so it will keep simmering. And stir it every once in a while.

5. While you're waiting for the sauce to cook, you can prepare the spaghetti. Just follow the directions in Step 1 of Basic Spaghetti on page 73.

6. Now you're just about ready to put everything to-gether. Put the spaghetti in a big warm serving bowl. (You can warm the bowl by running hot water in it and then wiping it dry just before you put the spaghetti in.) Make a little hollow in the middle of the spaghetti. Just press it down very lightly with a large spoon. Then pour the tomato sauce and meatballs over it.

7. Place the serving dish in front of your father at the table. I hope he can serve it without spilling anything on the tablecloth. Did he?

8. Don't forget the grated Parmesan cheese. Place it in a separate bowl so everyone can help himself.

SAM'S CHICKEN CHUNKS

This may be the world's easiest recipe. One nice thing about it, you can eat the chicken with your fingers—unless you're serving it for Sunday dinner or company. Or unless your parents object. In that case, mind your manners and use a knife and fork. Sam—he's ten years old—says it's his favorite thing to cook.

You will need:

> Cut up chicken (This comes in packages at the supermarket. ASK YOUR MOTHER HOW MUCH TO GET.)
> Butter or margarine
> Salt and pepper
> Dry mustard (Sam says this makes all the difference.)
> Parsley (This is just for decoration, so you can skip it if you want.)

1. Turn on the oven to 375 degrees.

2. Butter the bottom of a large baking pan and put the chicken pieces in it. Take some more butter (it's easier if you let it get a little soft) and rub it all over the tops of the chicken pieces.

3. Put about 3 tablespoons of salt into a little bowl. Then add about 1 tablespoon of black pepper and 1 teaspoon of dry mustard. Mix this all together with your fingers and then rub it over the top of each piece with your fingers. If you don't have enough, mix more.

4. Now put the chicken in the oven. That's all there is
to it. In 45 minutes, take it out of the oven. Put the
chicken chunks on a big platter and put them on the
dinner table. If you are feeling festive, decorate the platter with a few sprigs of parsley.

GOOD IDEA: Chicken chunks are particularly good
with Skinny Potatoes (the recipe is on page 86.) or rice
(just cook it as for Lazy Lucy's Wake-Up Rice on page
46,) and add some butter and salt and pepper.

KATY'S THROW-EVERYTHING-IN MEAT LOAF

My niece, Katy Cordes, started making meat loaf when
she was eight and a half years old. Her mother says she
uses everything in the refrigerator and it's never the same
twice, but it's always good. This is Katy's basic recipe.
Here's what you need:

    1½ pounds of ground beef
     1 egg
     1 cup of cornflakes or 1 cup of cold cooked
            rice or prepared poultry stuffing
     2 teaspoons salt
    ½ teaspoon pepper
     1 teaspoon thyme
    ½ green pepper
     1 medium can of tomatoes
     1 small can of tomato juice or a half cup of
            beef broth (You can make it with a
            bouillon cube.)
     1 small can of mushrooms (Get the cheapest
            can, the one that has stems in it. It tastes
            just as good.)
     3 onions

1. Now what you do is just throw everything into a big bowl.

2. But first cut the green pepper half into small pieces and throw away all the inside white part and seeds. Peel the onions and slice them up. IF YOU'VE NEVER PEELED AN ONION BEFORE, ASK YOUR MOTHER TO SHOW YOU HOW TO DO THE FIRST ONE. THEN YOU CAN DO THE OTHER TWO WHILE SHE WATCHES.

3. All right? Everything in the bowl? Now, I've told you often enough, wash your hands. This time it's important, because what you do is put your two hands right into that bowl and mess everything around until it's all mixed together.

4. Now wash your hands again. You better use a brush to get the meat loaf from under your fingernails.

5. Put the meat loaf in a pan. ASK YOUR MOTHER WHICH PAN TO USE. Put the pan in the oven. Turn the oven on to 350 degrees.

6. The meat loaf will be done in 1 hour and 15 minutes. If you like it crispy on top, leave it in another 15 minutes.

SUSAN'S FRENCH BEEF STEW

Susan is ten. She calls this French beef stew because it has red wine in it. If you use California wine, I suppose you could call it California Beef Stew. Susan won't mind. If you don't have any red wine, it really doesn't matter. You can use beef broth or water instead. It will still taste delicious. Stew tastes best if you make it one day and warm it up the next. Sitting around seems to make the flavor better.

Read the recipe all the way through and then get these things together:

       1½ pounds stew beef
       ¼ pound butter or margarine
       2 tablespoons flour
       ½ cup beef broth
       ½ cup red wine or beef broth or water
       3 onions
       4 cloves
       4 carrots
       1 bay leaf
       1 teaspoon thyme
       1 teaspoon salt
       ½ teaspoon pepper

1. Melt 4 tablespoons of butter in a big frying pan and put a few pieces of meat in at a time. Turn the meat around with a wooden spoon so it gets brown all over. When the meat is brown, put it in a casserole. You may need more butter to get all the meat brown. ASK YOUR MOTHER TO WATCH YOU WHILE YOU ARE BROWNING THE MEAT TO MAKE SURE YOU'RE DOING IT RIGHT. AND PLEASE BE CAREFUL, SO YOU WON'T GET BURNED.

2. When the meat is all browned and in the casserole, turn the heat off under the frying pan. Put 2 more tablespoons of butter into the frying pan. Now, add the 2 tablespoons of flour and rub it around in the butter with your wooden spoon until it is very smooth.

3. This is the hardest part: Add the half cup of beef broth to the flour and butter mixture very slowly and keep stirring it so there will be no lumps. It will get thick, but as you add more liquid it will get thin again. Turn the heat on under the frying pan—keep it very low—and stir

the whole thing around until its starts to bubble. (This is the way you made cream sauce, remember?) Then pour it in the casserole with the meat. If it is lumpy, you didn't do it right. You'll need more practice. But it doesn't really matter. The stew will taste good anyway.

4. Now pour the red wine into the frying pan. Swish it around and then pour it into the casserole.

5. Now peel 2 of the onions, cut them in quarters and put them in the casserole. CAREFUL WITH THAT KNIFE!

6. Peel the third onion. Take the 4 cloves and stick them into the onion and put the onion in the casserole.

7. Cut the tops and bottoms off the carrots and scrape them with the swivel-bladed peeler. MOTHER WILL PLEASE KEEP AN EAGLE EYE ON THE KNIFE WORK. Cut the carrots in two or three pieces and put them in the casserole. Put all the other ingredients in the casserole. Stir everything around a couple of times with your wooden spoon and put the cover on the casserole.

8. You can cook the stew on top of the stove over a very low heat for about 2 or 3 hours or you can put it in the oven at 300 degrees for about 2 or 3 hours.

9. Before you serve the stew, taste it to see if it needs a little more salt or pepper and take out the bay leaf and the onion with the cloves. Susan says this stew is very good with noodles.

SECOND-HELPING POT ROAST

This is a meal in itself—meat and vegetables and gravy galore. Of course, if you want to be elegant (and why not?) you refer to the gravy as sauce. Most people who

aren't on a diet or something will ask for a second helping. It's really that good.

You'll need:

> 4 pounds of beef (ASK YOUR MOTHER
>   WHAT CUT OF BEEF SHE PREFERS.
>   RUMP, SHOULDER, CHUCK AND
>   ROUND ARE ALL SUITABLE.)
> 2 tablespoons of flour
> 2 teaspoons of salt
> 4 tablespoons of butter or margarine (That's
>   half a stick.)
> 1 cup of red wine or beef broth (You can make
>   the broth with hot water and a bouillon
>   cube.)
> 6 to 8 black peppercorns
> 1 bay leaf
> 2 sprigs of parsley
> 1 large onion
> 2 or 3 cloves
> 1 cup of beef broth or water
> 6 carrots
> 6 potatoes
> 6 to 12 onions (The number depends on how
>   big the onions are and how much you like
>   them.)

1. Set the oven at 325 degrees and turn it on.

2. Mix the flour and salt together and rub it all over the
meat. Use your fingers, but, please, wash your hands first.

3. Get out the big black frying pan and melt the butter
in it. When it bubbles, put the meat in and let it brown.
Turn it so that it's brown on all sides. ASK YOUR
MOTHER TO STAND BY WHILE YOU'RE DOING
THIS.

4. When the meat is browned, put it in a deep casserole

or a Dutch oven that has a close-fitting cover. Then pour the cup of red wine into the frying pan. Stir it all around with a wooden spoon so that you'll get all the good brown bits off the bottom of the frying pan. Then pour the whole thing over the meat in the casserole.

5. Put the peppercorns, the bay leaf and the parsley in the casserole.

6. Peel the onion (IF YOU HAVEN'T HAD MUCH EXPERIENCE AT ONION-PEELING, PLEASE ASK YOUR MOTHER TO SEE THAT YOU DO IT CORRECTLY.) Stick the cloves into the peeled onion and then put it in the casserole.

7. Now add the cup of beef broth. Put the cover on the casserole and tuck it in the oven.

8. Let it cook for an hour. This would be a good time to do your homework. Then take the casserole out. BE CAREFUL, IT'S HOT. Turn the meat over and then put the casserole back in the oven for another hour.

9. While you're waiting, cut the tops and bottoms off the carrots and scrape them with a swivel-blade peeler. REMEMBER, WE'VE AGREED THAT WHEN YOU'RE WIELDING SHARP KNIVES AND SCRAPERS THERE SHOULD ALWAYS BE A PARENT AROUND TO SEE THAT YOU DO IT RIGHT. OKAY?

10. Peel the potatoes and put them in a pan of cold water.

11. Peel the onions. If you have time, you can do more homework.

12. When the casserole has been in the oven for 2 hours, add the carrots, potatoes and onions and let the whole thing cook until the vegetables are done. That should take about 30 to 45 minutes. ASK YOUR MOTHER TO HELP YOU CHECK WHEN THEY ARE READY.

13. I hope the table is set. You're just about ready to serve dinner. Take the meat out of the casserole and put it in the center of a warm platter. Fish out the vegetables and place them around the meat. But not that onion with the cloves in it. That was just for flavor. Throw it away. Or eat it, if you want. Just don't put it on the platter.

14. Strain the sauce that's left in the pan into a bowl. ASK YOUR MOTHER OR FATHER TO HELP. THAT CASSEROLE MUST BE HEAVY. Pour a little of the sauce over the meat on the platter and put the rest in a sauce boat to serve separately. It's time to eat!

SOMETHING GOOD TO KNOW: This is the kind of dish that tastes better the day after. If you want to make it the day before—say, for instance, you want to cook it on Saturday and serve it on Sunday—here's what you do: just follow the recipe right through Step 8. Then, let the pot roast cool and put it in the refrigerator overnight. This is a particularly good idea if someone in the family is trying to lose weight. Here's why: when you take it out of the refrigerator the next day, you'll find that all the fat has solidified on top and it's easy to lift it off and throw it away. After you've taken off the fat, warm up the casserole on the top of the stove or in a 325-degree oven. Then proceed with Step 9.

BASIC ROAST BEEF

I don't know one single person who doesn't like roast beef. It's one of the very best things for Sunday dinners or company dinners. It's easy to cook but people are always surprised when a kid tells them that he or she roasted it.

You'll need:

    4- to 5-pound rolled roast of beef (ASK YOUR
        MOTHER TO ORDER THE CUT SHE
        LIKES BEST.)
    1 onion
        Salt and pepper

1. Turn the oven on to 350 degrees.

2. Peel the onion and slice it. (IF YOU HAVEN'T DONE MUCH COOKING PLEASE ASK MOTHER TO STAND BY WHILE YOU OPERATE ON THE ONION.)

3. Put the onion slices on the bottom of the roasting pan and put the roast on top of the onion slices.

4. Now put some salt in the bottom of a little bowl— about 2 or 3 tablespoons—and then put about a tablespoon of pepper in the bowl. If you have a pepper mill, use that, because freshly ground pepper is pepperier. With your fingers, mix it all up (OH, OH, I FORGOT. I HOPE YOU WASHED YOUR HANDS.) and then rub it all over the top and sides of the roast.

5. Now stick a meat thermometer into the thickest part of the meat. ASK YOUR MOTHER TO SHOW YOU WHERE. Some people like their roast beef rare; some like it well done; some like it in between. The meat thermometer will show you when it has reached the stage you like.

6. Now put the roast in the oven. It should take about an hour. But keep your eye on the meat thermometer.

7. Some people like gravy. IF YOU WANT GRAVY, ASK YOUR MOTHER TO SHOW YOU HOW TO MAKE IT WHEN YOU TAKE THE ROAST OUT OF THE OVEN. In our family, we just like the good red juice that comes from the roast when it's cut.

GOOD IDEA: Serve this with Fancy Baked Potatoes (the recipe's on page 87) and people will think you are a very good cook. Well, you are.

SKINNY POTATOES

This is a good way to fix potatoes and make people think you've really been working. But you haven't, really. All you have to do is peel the potatoes and slice them.

You need:

> 1 potato for each person
> 1 tablespoon of butter or margarine for each
>   potato
> Salt and pepper

1. Turn the oven on to 500 degrees.

2. Peel the potatoes. (You did remember to wash your hands, didn't you?) We use a swivel-bladed vegetable peeler in our house. If you don't have one, use a sharp knife. BUT MAKE SURE YOU ASK YOUR MOTHER TO SHOW YOU HOW TO USE IT SO YOU WON'T CUT YOURSELF.

3. Slice the peeled potatoes into skinny slices. Well, not *too* skinny. About a quarter of an inch thick.

4. Butter the bottom of a shallow baking pan and place the potato slices very neatly in rows. If you have a big family, you may have to overlap the slices just a little bit to fit them in the pan.

5. Use up the rest of the butter by putting little pieces over the top of the potatoes, then put the pan in the oven.

6. After 10 minutes, take a spatula and move the pota-

toes around very gently just so they won't stick. Try not to break them. Then after another 10 minutes move them around again. After another 10 minutes, take them out of the oven, they'll be done.

7. Sprinkle some salt and pepper over them. They're ready to eat.

FANCY BAKED POTATOES

These are good for company. They're good without company, too.

You need:

    1 baking potato for each person
    2 tablespoons of butter for each potato
      Milk
      Salt and pepper
      Grated cheese
      Parsley (You don't really need it. It's just for looks.)

1. Turn the oven on to 450 degrees.

2. Wash the potatoes and put them in the oven. They will take about an hour to bake, depending on size. ASK YOUR MOTHER TO TELL YOU WHEN THEY'RE DONE.

3. When they're done, cut each potato in half the long way. WATCH OUT! THEY'RE HOT! Now take a spoon and scoop all the potato into a bowl. Be careful not to tear the skin.

4. Put the butter in the bowl and about half a cup of milk. Stir everything up. Maybe you'll need more milk. ASK YOUR MOTHER IF SHE THINKS YOU SHOULD PUT MORE MILK IN. The potato mixture should be a

little like mashed potatoes. If you have an electric mixer, you can mix the potatoes and butter and milk together with the mixer. BUT PLEASE ASK YOUR MOTHER TO WATCH WHILE YOU OPERATE THE MIXER. A wooden spoon is just as good. It just takes more energy.

5. Now, here's where the fun begins. Take a taste and then add a *little* salt and pepper. Take another taste. Does it need a little more salt and pepper? When it tastes the way you like it, give it two more stirs. Then with a spoon, put the potato mixture back in the potato skins.

6. Sprinkle a tiny bit of cheese over each potato half and then put them back in the oven for about 5 minutes so they'll be good and hot.

7. You can put a little sprig of parsley on top of each potato half.

BEGINNER'S BASIC SALAD KIT

Did you think I'd forgotten all about vegetables? I haven't, but I've been counting on your mother to see that you get all the good green and yellow vegetables you need. Most of the dishes you've learned to make in this chapter only need a green salad to turn them into a well-balanced meal. So here's the classic basic green salad. You can change it in a million ways (well, at least a thousand) to suit your own tastes. This is just what you might call a "beginner's basic salad kit."

You'll need:

> Greens (And I tell you frankly that if there's anything I despise, it's iceberg lettuce. There are so many other better kinds of greens. And most of them are better for you, too. When

you are choosing your salad greens, think of
Boston lettuce and Romaine and chicory and
watercress, even spinach. And there are lots
of others. Take a look around.)

Salad oil (This can be olive oil or corn oil or
safflower oil, whatever your mother keeps in
the kitchen cupboard.)

Vinegar (You can use cider vinegar, but I think
a good salad deserves a good red wine vinegar. No, it won't make you drunk. It's just for
flavor.)

Salt

Pepper (You should have learned by now that
there's a big difference in the taste of ready-
ground pepper and the pepper that you grind
yourself in your own pepper mill. The second
kind is better. Right?)

Mustard (The dry powder, not the kind you
spread on hot dogs.)

1. All right. That's the basic kit. Wash the greens that
you chose under cold running water. Do a good job. If
there's one thing that spoils a salad, it's sandy greens.
Ugh!

2. When the greens are clean (and how about your
hands?) shake them dry in a salad basket. If you don't
have one of those salad baskets that you can whirl around
to shake off the water, you can just pat the greens dry in a
clean dish towel. Then wrap them in another clean dish
towel and put them in the refrigerator until you're ready
to put the salad together.

3. Now, it's time for the creative part. Put 3 tablespoons of oil and 1 tablespoon of vinegar in a small
bowl. Add a pinch of mustard. (A pinch is just what
you can pick up between your thumb and finger.) Add
about a half teaspoon of salt and grind a little pepper in

to taste. Mix this up vigorously with a fork or a whisk—and there you are, salad dressing.

4. When you are more experienced, you will want to change the proportions of oil and vinegar to suit yourself. You might want to add a little lemon or some Worcestershire sauce—any number of things.

5. When you're ready to eat, put the greens in the salad bowl. You may want to tear the leaves into smaller pieces or leave them just as they are. Then add the salad dressing.

6. Now toss the salad. Tossing does *not* mean to throw it around. It means to turn it over and over with a salad fork and spoon until each bit of green is coated with the dressing.

FOR ADVANCED SALAD MAKERS: You can vary this basic salad by adding all sorts of things—chopped onions or chives, parsley, cucumbers, radishes, tomatoes, green peppers, celery. You can also turn it into a hot-weather supper by adding cut-up chicken or shrimp or slivers of ham and cheese, or sliced eggs or sardines or tuna fish or . . . I don't think anyone has ever counted all the possible variations on a basic salad. Do you want to try?

GOOD OLD SPINACH

Mothers used to tell children, "Eat your spinach. It's good for you. It's full of iron." And so it is, but scientists have discovered that the kind of iron that's in spinach is not easily absorbed by the body. So it's not all that good for you. However, it does contain something called carotene, which turns into vitamin A after you eat it—and that's good for you.

Besides, spinach tastes good. It's particularly tasty with the meat and spaghetti dishes in this chapter.

Here's how you cook it. Get together:

> 2 pounds of fresh spinach (That's enough for four people. And fresh spinach is so much better than frozen spinach that it's laughable.)
> Butter
> Salt
> Pepper (Grind it yourself, please.)
> Nutmeg (If your mother has a whole nutmeg and a nutmeg grinder, you're in luck. If not, the regular nutmeg out of the little box will do.)

1. Wash the spinach. This is the only hard part. You'll need at least three separate cold-water washings to get all the sand out of the spinach. While you're washing it, cut off the thick stem ends so that you'll just have the good green leaves.

2. When you're positive that you've got all the sand out, shake the water off the spinach and put it in a pan. Don't put any water in the pan. Sprinkle a little salt—just a little—over the leaves and turn on the heat.

3. Spinach takes about 5 minutes to cook, once the water from the leaves starts to boil. You can stir it around a little if you want. When the leaves are all limp and tender, it's done.

4. Now measure out a quarter of a teaspoon of nutmeg and sprinkle it over the spinach. Stir it around.

5. Drain the spinach in the colander. ASK YOUR MOTHER TO HELP. I DON'T WANT YOU TO GET SCALDED.

6. Put the spinach in a bowl. Add a couple of tablespoons of butter, a little more salt and some pepper. Keep

tasting it to see just how much salt and pepper you want. REMEMBER, EASY DOES IT. It's easy enough to add salt, but it's impossible to take it out. Perhaps it needs just a smidgen more butter. What do you think?

7. Okay. It's just right. Put it on the table.

HOT BUTTERED JUICE

You've learned how to cook all sorts of main dishes. Here's a first course to serve before you put them on the table. A first course should be light so it won't spoil people's appetites. In fact, many people call the first course an appetizer. This vitamin C cocktail is a good introduction to a meal.

Here's how you make it. Get out:

    1 medium can of tomato juice
    2 or 3 tablespoons of butter
    1 teaspoon of Worcestershire sauce
    2 tablespoons of chopped chives or the green
        part of scallions

1. Put the tomato juice, butter and Worcestershire sauce in a pan and heat it until it boils.

2. Pour it (CAREFUL, NOW!) into small soup bowls or bouillon cups or mugs and sprinkle the chives over the top.

3. Serve it while it's piping hot.

EXTRA: If you want to make this really hot, add a few drops of Tabasco. BUT WATCH IT, TOO MUCH TABASCO CAN MAKE YOU FEEL AS IF YOU HAD A FIRE INSIDE.

SUMMER AND WINTER

FOUR

A BAKER'S DOZEN
of
SUMMER COOLERS
and
VACATION PROJECTS

Summertime is "when the livin' is easy." It's paper plate time, cook-out time, picnic time. For the cook, summer should be a treat. It's the time of the freshest vegetables, of berries and fruits, of seafood straight from the ocean. It's time to splurge on a Billion-Dollar Lobster Roll and sip Shivering Cold Lemonade. It's a time to entertain at a Caveman Steak cook-out. It's a time to have a project—like learning how to bake your own bread. Most of all, summertime is a time for the family to enjoy life together.

L-O-B-S-T-E-R SPELLS SUMMER

Or, you could say that S-U-M-M-E-R spells lobster. But no matter how mixed up your spelling is, there's one sure thing—lobster is one of summer's treats. If you live by the ocean, you can boil your lobster in a kettle of salty sea water. If you don't, here's what you do.

You'll need:

> Water
> 10 peppercorns
> 3 heaping tablespoons of salt
> 4 1½-pound lobsters (Fresh, fresh, fresh! Make
> sure they're lively.)

1. Take a big kettle and fill it with enough water to cover the lobsters. Add the peppercorns and salt. Put it on the stove and wait for it to boil. (If you use sea water, don't add anything. There's enough good salty flavor already in it. OF COURSE, YOU WON'T USE SEA WATER IF THERE'S BEEN ANY DANGER OF POLLUTION. THAT WOULD BE ASKING FOR TROUBLE.)

2. When the water is boiling hard, plunge the live lobsters in. Head and claws first. PLEASE ASK YOUR MOTHER OR FATHER TO HELP YOU. YOU DON'T WANT THOSE LOBSTERS TO PINCH YOU. AND YOU DON'T WANT TO GET SCALDED BY THAT BOILING WATER. No, it doesn't hurt the lobsters. I promise you. Experts tell me that they lose consciousness immediately.

3. Cover the kettle and let the lobsters cook for a good 15 minutes after the water has come back to a boil. (By "a good 15 minutes," I mean 15 or 16 or even 17 minutes. The point is that your lobsters probably won't be exactly

1½ pounds each. If they weigh a couple of ounces more, they should cook just a tiny bit more.)

4. ASK WHICHEVER PARENT IS NEAREST TO HELP YOU TAKE THE LOBSTERS OUT OF THE KETTLE. Take the smallest one out first. Put them in the kitchen sink. (I hope there aren't any dirty dishes in the sink.)

5. Let them drain for a minute or two. Turn them over so as much water as possible will drain out. WATCH YOUR FINGERS, THEY'RE HOT! Now they're ready to eat. YOUR MOTHER OR FATHER WILL SHOW YOU HOW TO CRACK THE CLAWS AND SPLIT THE BODY. You can serve them with melted butter or mayonnaise or cocktail sauce—whatever you like. But I recommend Green and Yellow Sauce. It's the next recipe.

NOTE: You might cook a couple of extra lobsters and let them cool so you can use them to make Billion-Dollar Lobster Rolls. You'll find the $$$$$$$$$ Lobster Rolls on page 98. Each dollar sign represents a hundred million dollars. So how many millions make up a billion? The answer is— Oh, why should I make it easy for you? You'll find the answer in the $$$$$$$$$ Lobster Roll recipe.

GREEN AND YELLOW SAUCE

Melted butter is very good with lobster, but melted butter and lemon juice is better. And melted butter and lemon juice and chives and . . . is even better.

You'll need:

> ¼ pound of butter
>
> 2 teaspoons of lemon juice (If you like tart flavors, you may want to add more lemon juice, but try it this way first.)
>
> 2 drops of Tabasco sauce (And that's plenty. Tabasco is very hot.)
>
> ½ teaspoon of Worcestershire sauce
>
> 1 tablespoon of finely chopped parsley (DO I STILL HAVE TO TELL YOU TO BE CAREFUL WITH THAT KNIFE?)
>
> 1 tablespoon (or maybe a little more) of finely chopped chives (OKAY, BE CAREFUL, DON'T CHOP YOUR FINGERS.)

1. Melt the butter over low heat. Be careful, you don't want it to bubble. Just let it melt slowly.

2. While the butter is melting, warm the bowls or little dishes or whatever you're going to serve the sauce in. Run hot water over them and wipe them dry. Or place them on the sunny windowsill.

3. When the butter is melted, take the pan off the stove and add the rest of the ingredients. Stir everything around with a fork. That's all there is to it.

NOTE: This sauce is so good that you may have to make a second batch. But that's all right. It's easy.

BILLION-DOLLAR LOBSTER ROLL

A billionaire couldn't ask for anything better. It's especially good when the temperature's so high no one feels like lifting a finger. Serve it with Shivering Cold Lemonade.

You'll need:

3 tablespoons of salad oil

1 tablespoon of vinegar (If your mother has white wine vinegar, that's best for this recipe, but red wine vinegar is perfectly good.)

Salt

Pepper (And now, you people who have been cooking your way through this book, what's the best kind of pepper? You're right. Freshly ground pepper from your own pepper mill.)

2 tablespoons of chili sauce or ketchup

½ cup of mayonnaise

2 tablespoons of chopped parsley (BE CAREFUL. THE POINT IS TO CHOP THE PARSLEY, NOT YOUR FINGERNAILS.)

2 tablespoons of chopped scallions (Just chop the green parts. Incidentally, if you want, you can just snip, snip, snip the scallions with the kitchen scissors.)

⅔ cup of chopped celery (Use the inside pieces. The easiest way to do this is to slice the stalks lengthwise into three or four thin strips and then chop those.)

2 cups (or more) of lobster meat (This should be cut or torn into bite-size pieces.)

4 hamburger rolls (or use French bread or seeded rolls. Use your imagination.)

8 lettuce leaves (Use Boston lettuce. Some people call it native lettuce. Or use Romaine. Any of the broad-leaved lettuces are good. But forget about iceberg lettuce. It just doesn't have that good green flavor.)

1. Mix the oil and vinegar, half a teaspoon of salt and half a teaspoon of pepper, together with a fork.

2. Now stir in everything else except the rolls and the

lettuce. Mix it up well, but be gentle. Try not to mash the lobster.

3. You'll like this part: Taste it to see if it needs more salt or pepper. Perhaps you'd like to add a little more mayonnaise or chili sauce. Adjust it to suit your taste.

4. Split the rolls and toast them split-side-up under the broiler. A PARENT SHOULD STAND BY WHILE YOU USE THE BROILER.

5. Put a lettuce leaf on four of the halves. Then put a quarter of the lobster mixture on each lettuce leaf. Pat it down gently. Cover it with another lettuce leaf and then with the other half of the roll.

6. Delicious! Put a few potato chips on each plate. And perhaps a few slices of ripe red tomato.

ARITHMETIC NOTE: Did you figure out how many millions there were in a billion? One thousand.

DIPPY SHRIMP

There's something about summer that makes food you eat in your fingers extra good. Maybe it's because nobody feels like doing dishes. (Of course, I don't know anyone who feels like doing dishes in the winter either.) Dippy Shrimp should probably be eaten outdoors, because the whole thing can get plenty messy.

You'll need:

3 pounds of shrimp
1 onion
1 quart of water (The easiest way to measure
    this is with a milk bottle or carton. Or use
    a cup. You do know there are four cups in a
    quart, don't you?
1 teaspoon of salt
8 peppercorns
Juice of half a lemon

1. Wash the shrimp. All you have to do is put them in a colander and jiggle them around a bit under cold running water.

2. Peel the onion. You ought to be an expert on onions by now. Then cut it in quarters. And while you're about it, wash your hands.

3. Put everything except the shrimp into a large pan and put the pan on the stove.

4. When the water boils, add the shrimp. BE CARE-FUL. A PARENT SHOULD KEEP AN EYE ON THIS. When the water starts boiling again, let the shrimp cook for 3 or 4 minutes, depending on their size. ASK YOUR MOTHER WHAT SHE THINKS.

5. Drain the shrimp in the colander, then put them in a large bowl in the middle of the table where everyone can reach them.

6. Serve Yellow and Green Sauce with them. That's the same one you used for the lobster. PERHAPS YOUR MOTHER COULD MAKE THE SAUCE WHILE YOU COOK THE SHRIMP. Peel your shrimp, then pick it up by its tail. Dip it in the sauce and then—transfer it to your mouth.

PETE'S TOWER OF PISA

When it's 90° in the shade, no one likes to cook. But people still get hungry. You'll be the family hero if you put this cool club sandwich together. Pete called his version the Tower of Pisa because it has Italian salami in it and it's so tall that it leans.

You need:

    12 slices of white or whole wheat toast
        Mayonnaise
     8 lettuce leaves
    16 strips of cooked bacon
     2 ripe tomatoes
     8 slices of chicken
     4 slices of boiled ham
        Potato chips
    16 slices of cucumber
     8 slices of Italian salami

1. Spread one side of each piece of toast with mayonnaise. Put a leaf of lettuce on each of four slices of toast. Then add four strips of bacon to each.

2. Slice the tomatoes and arrange them over the bacon. Put a slice of chicken over the tomatoes. Add another slice of toast, the mayonnaise-side down. Then spread mayonnaise on the other side.

3. Put a slice of ham on, then cover the ham with another slice of chicken. Make a layer of potato chips over the chicken. And then put four slices of cucumber on each stack. They should be getting pretty high.

4. Add 2 pieces of salami to each and cover with 1 piece of lettuce. Top off each tower with a piece of toast.

5. Cut them in half diagonally. BE CAREFUL. TRY TO HOLD EACH SANDWICH SO THE INSIDES WON'T SPILL OUT. I SUGGEST YOU ASK YOUR MOTHER TO HELP YOU. Use toothpicks to hold your Towers of Pisa together.

NOTE: You can get everything ready in the morning before it gets really hot and then build your sandwiches just before you're ready to eat.

GRATE CHICKEN

Grate Chicken is really great. Toasty and crunchy on the outside, juicy on the inside. It's cooked on a grate over white-hot glowing coals. This is a good project for fathers and sons. It's a good project for mothers and sons, fathers and daughters, and mothers and daughters, too.

You'll need:

2 2- to 3-pound broiling chickens (Have them cut in half so you'll have four pieces.)
A large flat rock or a wooden mallet
½ cup of salad oil
Salt and pepper

1. Start your fire. (AND, OF COURSE, A PARENT SHOULD CONSENT AND ADVISE.) It takes a while. Then go get everything together in the kitchen, put it in a basket or on a large tray and carry it out to the grill.

2. Put the chicken on a flat surface, skin-side up. Pound it a couple of times with the rock or mallet. This will make it lie flat on the grate and cook evenly.

3. Rub the chicken all over with the oil. Use your fingers. It's easier. WASH THEM FIRST!

4. Now wipe your hands on a paper towel. I suppose it's too much to expect you to go in and wash them again. Sprinkle both sides of the chicken with salt and pepper. (As I keep saying, use pepper ground from a pepper mill.)

5. When the fire is ready—the coals should have turned from red-hot to white-hot—put the chicken on the grate, skin-side up. Cook for 10 minutes and then turn and cook on the other side for about 10 minutes. ASK YOUR FATHER OR MOTHER EXACTLY HOW LONG TO COOK THE CHICKEN. IT DEPENDS ON HOW BIG

IT IS AND HOW CLOSE THE GRILL IS TO THE COALS. Perhaps you should turn it again and cook it another 5 minutes on each side.

CAVEMAN STEAK

Cavemen used to throw chunks of meat into the fire and then drag them out with a stick. This is a twentieth-century version. It uses chunks of steak and sticks, but the cavemen never had it so good.

You'll need:

> 2 pounds of beef (ASK YOUR MOTHER WHAT SHE SUGGESTS. IT SHOULD BE LEAN BEEF. Ask the butcher to cut it into two-inch cubes for you.)
> 3 tablespoons of red wine vinegar
> 2 tablespoons of lemon juice
> ¼ cup of salad oil
> ½ cup of orange juice
> 1 sliced onion
> ½ teaspoon of dry mustard
> 2 teaspoons of salt
> 1 teaspoon of black pepper
> 2 green peppers
> 2 or 3 onions
> 12 cherry tomatoes
> 1 zucchini
> 6 long barbecue skewers

YOU HAVE TO START CAVEMAN STEAK THE NIGHT BEFORE. HERE'S WHAT YOU DO:

1. Put the meat, vinegar, lemon juice, oil, orange juice, sliced onion, mustard, salt and pepper in a large bowl. Stir it all up. Make sure the meat is well coated. Cover the bowl with a piece of aluminum foil and put it in the refrigerator. That's all for now.

ON BARBECUE DAY:

1. Stir the meat around a couple of times during the day. About an hour before you want to start cooking take the meat out of the refrigerator.

2. Start the fire in the grill. You'll need white-hot coals to cook this. AND I KNOW THAT I DON'T HAVE TO TELL YOU THAT YOU DON'T BUILD FIRES OR BARBECUE WITHOUT ADULT SUPERVISION.

3. Wash the green peppers and cut each one into six even pieces. Scrape the white part and seeds off.

4. Peel the onions and slice them. You need 12 rather thick slices. IF YOU ARE NOT AN EXPERT ONION-SLICER, YOUR MOTHER SHOULD KEEP AN EYE ON THE OPERATION.

5. Wash the cherry tomatoes.

6. Wash the zucchini. Cut off the ends and then slice it into six equal pieces.

7. This part is fun. Divide everything into six piles. Then start threading the skewers. Start with a piece of beef, then a slice of onion, then beef, then a tomato and so on.

8. Put the skewers on a platter and brush some of the marinade over them. (The marinade is the liquid it was soaking in all night.)

9. You can start cooking whenever the fire is ready. The skewers should be about four inches from the coals. Keep turning them so everything will cook evenly. Fifteen minutes should just about do it.

THERE'S POTATO SALAD

And thank goodness. I don't know what we'd do in summer without it. This goes with almost every summer meal. And if you want to serve the easiest meal of all, just give people some cold sliced meat—chicken or beef or ham or cold cuts—with potato salad and some sliced tomatoes. Cool! Delicious! Easy!

You'll need:

    1½ pounds of potatoes
        Salt
    2 hard-boiled eggs (Turn back to page 62 for the right way to cook eggs.)
    3 tablespoons of salad oil
    1 tablespoon of red wine vinegar
    ½ teaspoon of pepper (Ground with your own pepper mill, of course.)
    2 red onions (If you can't get red ones, use the everyday yellow ones.)
    3 tablespoons of chopped parsley (REMEMBER, YOU'RE CHOPPING PARSLEY, NOT GIVING YOURSELF A MANICURE.)
    ¼ cup of mayonnaise (or a little more if you like)

1. Wash the potatoes and put them in boiling water with a little salt in it. Oh, about a teaspoon of salt. Cook the potatoes until they are just tender. ASK YOUR MOTHER HOW LONG. IT DEPENDS ON HOW LARGE THEY ARE.

2. Drain the potatoes in a colander. And when they're cool enough to handle, peel them. The skin comes off very easily. Now, slice them neatly and put them in a bowl.

3. Cut the eggs in quarters and add to the potatoes.

4. Mix the salad oil, vinegar, a sprinkle of salt and a grind of pepper together in a bowl.

5. Peel the red onions (CAREFUL WITH THAT KNIFE!) and slice them. Pick the onion rings apart and

add them to the oil and vinegar. Now add the parsley and mayonnaise. Mix everything together and then pour it over the potatoes and eggs.

6. Stir everything around gently, then put your potato salad in the refrigerator until you're ready to eat.

SIXTEEN-MINUTE BLUEBERRY CHEESECAKE

You won't be able to put this together in sixteen minutes the first time. But with a little practice, you will. Maybe you can make it even faster. Be sure to read the recipe all the way through before you start. (You do that with every recipe, don't you?)

You'll need:

    2 tablespoons of cold water
    2 tablespoons of lemon juice
    1 envelope of gelatine (the unflavored kind)
    ½ cup milk
    2 egg yolks (HAVE YOU SEPARATED YOLKS FROM WHITES BEFORE? THERE'S A KNACK TO IT. ASK YOUR MOTHER TO SHOW YOU HOW SHE DOES IT. SHE CAN DO ONE EGG AND YOU CAN DO THE OTHER. SAVE THE EGG WHITES. YOU CAN ADD THEM TO SCRAMBLED EGGS.)
    ⅓ cup of sugar
    2 cups of creamed cottage cheese
    1 crumby crust (This doesn't count in the sixteen minutes. The next recipe tells you how to make it. See why you always have to read recipes through?)
    ½ cup currant jelly
    1 pint of blueberries washed and picked over so there aren't any stems or little green berries

YOU USE AN ELECTRIC BLENDER TO MAKE THIS CHEESECAKE. SO LET'S MAKE A RULE, RIGHT HERE AND NOW: YOU DO NOT USE AN ELECTRIC BLENDER UNLESS YOUR MOTHER OR YOUR FATHER IS THERE TO KEEP AN EYE ON THINGS—OR UNLESS YOU HAVE BEEN GIVEN PERMISSION BY YOUR PARENTS. OKAY?

1. Put the first three ingredients—water, lemon juice and gelatin—into the blender. Cover and blend at low speed.

2. Put the milk in a small pan and heat it to the boiling point. Then pour it in the blender, which is still on low.

3. When the gelatin is dissolved (when you can't see the separate little grains any more) turn the blender to high and add the egg yolks, the sugar and the cottage cheese. Keep blending until they're smooth. Then turn off the blender.

4. Pour the whole thing into the crumby crust. All right, how long did it take you? Now your cheesecake goes in the refrigerator for 2 hours.

5. When 2 hours are almost up, melt the currant jelly over very low heat in a small pan. Stir it so it will be smooth and then put it aside for a few minutes to cool.

6. When the jelly is cool, add the blueberries and stir them around until each is coated with jelly.

7. Spoon the blueberries evenly over the top of the cheesecake. Then put it back in the refrigerator for 15 minutes. You can leave it in much longer, of course. Just keep it there until you're ready to serve it.

NOTE: If you look in one of your mother's cookbooks,

you'll probably find a lot of things to do with leftover egg whites. Be sure you don't waste them.

CRUMBLY PIE CRUST

This is really a cinch to make. You can use it for pies (chocolate-pudding pie is especially good in crumbly crust) as well as cheesecake.

You'll need:

> 18 to 20 graham crackers
> ¼ cup of butter (Let it get soft before you start.)
> ¼ cup of sugar
> ¼ teaspoon of cinnamon

1. Put the graham crackers between two dish towels or two pieces of wax paper and roll them into crumbs with the rolling pin. Or put the crackers, a few at a time, into the blender. (REMEMBER THE BLENDER RULE. IF YOU DON'T REMEMBER IT, GO BACK TO PAGE 108 AND READ IT.) Turn the blender on high and whirl the crackers into crumbs.

2. Now put the crumbs and everything else into a bowl. Wash your hands and mix it all up with your fingers.

3. When it sticks together, put it in a 9-inch pie plate and press it evenly all over the bottom and sides of the pie plate. Don't try to put it on the rim.

4. That's all there is to it. Put it in the refrigerator until your cheesecake mixture is ready.

SHIVERING COLD LEMONADE

When we used to go to Connecticut on the train, there was a man who walked up and down the aisle and sold ice cream and cold drinks. He would call out, "Get your shivering cold drinks here." That's how this lemonade got its name. And it is shivering cold. B-r-r-r!

This is a two-step recipe.

You'll need:

      ½ cup of freshly squeezed lemon juice
      2 cups of water
      ½ cup of sugar

1. Mix this together well. Stir it until the sugar is dissolved and then pour it into an ice-cube tray and put it in the freezing compartment.

When your lemonade ice cubes are ready, you'll need:

      ½ cup of freshly squeezed lemon juice
      2 cups of cold, cold water
      ½ cup of sugar
      Mint leaves (These are nice for decoration,
        but you don't *really* need them.)

1. Mix the juice and water and sugar together. Stir until the sugar is dissolved.

2. Now take a sip. Perhaps you would like a little more sugar. Or is it just right?

3. Get out four tall glasses and put three or four lemonade ice cubes in each glass. Now fill the glasses with lemonade. Float a mint leaf or two on top. Drink. This is the best and coldest lemonade ever.

NOTE ONE: You can double or triple the first part of

this recipe. Then, when your lemonade cubes are frozen, put them in plastic bags and keep them in the freezer. They'll be ready whenever you're thirsty.

NOTE TWO: If you want to be fancy, you can freeze a mint leaf or a maraschino cherry or a small piece of lemon peel in your lemonade cubes. Here's how you do it. Make your lemonade cube mixture. Pour half of it into the ice-cube tray. When it has frozen so that it's kind of mushy, place a mint leaf or cherry on top of each cube, then pour the rest of the lemonade mixture over it and put the tray back in the freezer. Can you think of other ways to make the lemonade cubes interesting?

MUSCLEMAN BREAD

Learning to bake bread is a good vacation project. Once you know how to work with a yeast dough (did you know yeast was alive?), there are many other good things you can make. Sweet breakfast rolls and German Christmas bread full of fruit and nuts. And pretzels. And sourdough bread like the early pioneers and miners baked in the Wild West.

Why bother to bake bread at all? Because home-baked bread is the best of all; there are no chemicals added to it to make it stay fresh longer. Home-baked bread tastes so good it never has a chance to get stale. Incidentally, boys are particularly good at making bread. It gives them a chance to use their muscles. Maybe that's why most bakers are men.

Be sure to read this recipe through carefully before you start.

You'll need:

3 cups of warm water (And I mean warm, not
    hot. It should be just a little warmer than
    your skin.)
3 tablespoons of sugar
3 cakes of yeast (You can use the packages of
    dry yeast, but I like yeast cakes because
    they smell so good and it's fun to crumble
    them up.)
3 teaspoons of salt
1 cup of wheat germ (If you don't have wheat
    germ in the house, substitute a cup of
    flour.)
8 cups of flour (You may need a little more or
    a little less.)
3 tablespoons of corn oil or melted butter

THIS IS AN EASY RECIPE TO REMEMBER. EV-
ERYTHING COMES IN THREES EXCEPT THE
WHEAT GERM AND THE FLOUR. AND IF YOU
ADD THEM TOGETHER, WELL, THEY MAKE
THREE TIMES THREE.

1. Get out a very big bowl, the largest mixing bowl in
the cupboard. Measure the water and the sugar into it.
Then add the yeast. Crumble the yeast cakes between
your fingers as you add them. (Don't you like that yeasty
smell?)

2. Now get out a sturdy wooden spoon and stir until
the yeast is dissolved.

3. Add the salt, the wheat germ and three cups of flour
and stir like mad. When everything is well mixed to-
gether, beat it up until the batter is nice and smooth.
BEATING IS DIFFERENT FROM STIRRING. STIR-
RING IS A ROUND AND ROUND MOTION. BEAT-
ING IS MORE LIKE DOWN AND UNDER AND UP
AND OVER. ASK YOUR MOTHER TO DEMON-

STRATE. About 2 minutes of beating should be enough. I'm sure you'll think it's enough.

4. Add the oil and then start adding the rest of the flour—1 cup at a time. Mix each cup of flour into the batter before you add the next one. It gets harder and harder. Ask for help if it gets too hard for you. But do as much as you can yourself.

5. When you add the last cup of flour, the dough should hold together pretty well. It will be just a little sticky, but not very. ASK YOUR MOTHER IF SHE THINKS IT'S READY TO KNEAD. It's important to remember that it's better to add too little flour than too much, especially when you're a beginner. You can always add more flour when you knead the dough. But if you add too much, there's no way to take it out.

6. If your kitchen table or counter has a Formica top, sprinkle a little flour on it and then scrape the bread dough out of the bowl onto the flour. OR YOUR MOTHER MAY HAVE A PASTRY BOARD. ASK HER ADVICE ABOUT WHAT YOU SHOULD WORK ON.

7. Wash the empty bowl. And dry it, please. Then butter the inside. When you finish kneading the dough, you're going to pop it right back into the bowl, so you might as well have it ready.

8. Now the dough is supposed to "rest" for 5 minutes. So while it's resting, perhaps you'd like to know what's been happening to it. First of all, when you mixed the water and the yeast and the sugar together you set up a little yeast factory. The warm water and sugar made the yeast cells start to grow. Did you know that yeast is alive? Well, it is. It's a primitive form of plant and it started growing bigger and multiplying in the warm water. It also started to make carbon dioxide gas. It's still doing

this—right there on the kitchen table. Pretty soon, you'll be able to see the way the gas makes your dough expand. The dough will get bigger and bigger until it's twice the size it is now. All the tiny gas bubbles will push the dough up and make it light and airy instead of tough and heavy. All right, the dough has had a chance to rest. And so have you. Let's get back to work.

9. Stick your hands in the flour and get them all white and floury. This will help you handle the dough without it sticking to your fingers. Now you're ready to knead.

10. The first thing you do is push the dough that's been resting into a round shape. KNEADING TAKES A LOT OF ENERGY. BUT IT'S A LOT OF FUN. ASK YOUR MOTHER TO SHOW YOU HOW TO DO IT. IF YOU WATCH HER CAREFULLY, YOU'LL SEE THAT THERE'S A KIND OF RHYTHM ABOUT IT. SO IF YOU FEEL LIKE WHISTLING WHILE YOU WORK, PICK A TUNE THAT MATCHES THE KNEADING RHYTHM. JUST IN CASE MOTHER HAS NEVER BAKED A LOAF OF BREAD AND DOESN'T KNOW HOW TO KNEAD, HERE ARE SOME BASIC IN-STRUCTIONS: BOTH OF YOU CAN EXPERIMENT TOGETHER.

Here's what you do: Press the round ball of dough flat, then pick up the edge that's farthest away from you and fold it over toward you. Now press the heels of your hand into the dough so that you're flattening the dough down and pushing it away from you at the same time.

Now pick the dough up and turn it a quarter circle around and repeat—folding the farther edge over toward you and then pushing the dough down and away with the heels of your hands. After you repeat this three or four times, you'll begin to develop a rhythm. You'll find that each time you pick up the dough to turn it a quarter of a circle, you'll slap it down hard on the table. Don't be afraid to use plenty of muscle. When the dough gets too sticky, put a little more flour on your hands and on the board or table.

Kneading takes about 10 minutes. After a while, the dough starts to look really smooth and it gets easier to handle. Then, it gets little "stretch blisters" and that means it's about ready. But give it a good 10 minutes.

11. Now, shape the dough into a tidy ball and put it in a buttered bowl. Turn it around in the bowl so that the dough is buttery all over. Cover the bowl with plastic wrap and a clean dish towel and put it in a warm spot where there are no drafts. The yeast has to have a chance to do its work now. The bread will rise best in a temperature between 80 and 90 degrees. If your oven has a gas pilot light, the oven would be a good warm place to put your bread bowl. ASK YOUR MOTHER WHAT SHE SUGGESTS.

12. Before you start relaxing after all that kneading, wipe off the kitchen table or the counter where you worked and wash your cooking dishes. It's always easier to clean things up as you go along.

13. In an hour, take a look at the dough. Has it doubled? If it hasn't cover it up again and tuck it back into its warm place. Check again in 15 minutes. If you think it has just about doubled, here's how to test it to be sure: Stick your finger in the dough. Gently, now. Just make a hole about half an inch deep. Now wait a couple of minutes. If the hole starts to fill up, the dough is still rising. But if the hole just stays there, then the dough has completed its first rising.

14. This step is fun. You make a fist and sock the bread.

It will collapse very satisfactorily. If you listen, you can hear it go whoosh as the gas bubbles escape.

15. Turn the dough out on a floured working place again and knead it for a couple of minutes. Then put it back in its bowl and let it rise again. Cover the bowl just the way you did before and put it in the same warm spot.

16. There are more yeast cells now, so the bread will rise faster this time. It will only take about half the time to double itself. While you're waiting you might as well butter your bread pans. You have enough dough to fill two large bread pans or three medium ones.

17. When your bread has completed its second rising, turn the dough out on your floured working surface. Divide the dough in two or three parts depending on whether you're using two or three bread pans. Roll each portion into a tidy ball and put it in a bread pan. Some people make a big deal about shaping the loaf, but if you just press the dough down into the pan firmly but gently, so that it reaches all the corners, that's all you need to do. The bread takes care of itself very nicely, thank you.

18. Put the pans in a warm place. Cover them with a clean dish towel. Wait for the loaves to double. It won't take very long this time.

19. Turn the oven on to 400 degrees while you're waiting.

20. When the loaves are doubled, put them in the oven and bake for 40 to 45 minutes.

21. When they're done, take them out. BE CAREFUL. USE TWO THICK POT HOLDERS. Turn the bread out on a wire rack and let it cool.

22. If you're not quite sure whether the bread is completely baked, here's what you do: Knock on the bottom of the loaf. That's right. Just knock gently. It should

sound hollow. If it doesn't, just pop the bread back in its pan and let it bake a little longer.

NOTE ONE: Don't try to slice bread before it has cooled, no matter how good it smells or how hungry you are. It will just get all mashed together and doughy. Wait.

NOTE TWO: Bread is a good present—when you're a weekend visitor, for instance, or for Christmas. Especially if you wrap it with a little jar of your own homemade jam. (There's a recipe for that on this page.) All your uncles and aunts and grandparents and neighbors will think you're something special to have baked a loaf of bread just for them. I think you are, too.

NOTE THREE: If you feel like it, get some of the small aluminum-foil bread pans. This recipe will make about a dozen very small loaves. These loaves are particularly good for making fancy sandwiches or for presents. Just remember, they don't have to bake as long as the big loaves. About 20 minutes should be enough.

GOOD IDEA: When you get to Step 10, divide the dough into two or three parts (depending on how many people are cooking along) before you start kneading. The Junior and Senior Cooks can each knead half of the dough. This is a lot easier than kneading the whole batch by yourself.

YOUR OWN HOMEMADE STRAWBERRY JAM

There's something very sensible about the way summer vacation and the strawberry season go together. And the blueberry season. And the raspberry season. And the blackberry season. If you spend your vacation someplace where you can pick your own berries, making jam is a way of keeping a little bit of vacation all year round. But if you can't pick your own berries, you can buy them and still have your very own taste of summer to spread on your toast in the winter.

You'll need:

1 quart of strawberries
3 cups of sugar
4 or 5 glass jelly or jam jars with covers
   Paraffin (This is a wax that you melt to seal the jam away from germs. You can usually buy it at the supermarket or the hardware store.)

1. Making jam is really very easy. You start by hulling the strawberries, that is, taking off the green part at the stem end. You can do this with your fingers.

2. Then put the berries and 1 cup of sugar in a big pan and put it on the stove over low heat. Stir the berries and sugar very carefully. Try not to crush the berries. When your jam starts boiling, keep stirring, but also keep an eye on the clock. It should boil for exactly 3 minutes.

3. Then add another cup of sugar. Keep stirring. When it starts to boil again, let it boil for another 3 minutes.

4. Add the last cup of sugar and let it all boil for 3 more minutes while you keep stirring gently. Then turn off the heat. If there's any foam on top, skim it off with a big spoon.

5. Pour the jam into a shallow dish or bowl and let it cool.

6. While it's cooling, you can sterilize your jam jars. PLEASE BE SURE THAT YOUR MOTHER OR FATHER IS AROUND WHILE YOU DO THIS. I'D HATE

FOR YOU TO GET SCALDED WITH BOILING WATER. Wash the jars and lids in hot soapy water. Rinse them carefully in clear water so they are very clean. Now put them in a large pan of cold water on the stove. Turn the heat on, but keep it low so the water will heat slowly. When the water boils, turn the heat lower so that it will just simmer. Let it simmer for 10 to 12 minutes. Use tongs to take the jars out one at a time. ASK YOUR MOTHER OR FATHER TO HELP YOU DO THIS.

7. Spoon the jam into the sterilized jars.

8. Put the paraffin in a small pan and set the small pan in a large pan of water. Turn on the heat and wait until the paraffin has melted. PARENTS SHOULD KEEP AN EYE ON THIS PART OF THE OPERATION. IN FACT, IT MIGHT BE A GOOD IDEA IF THEY DID IT. HOT PARAFFIN CAN GIVE A PERSON A NASTY BURN. When it's melted pour a little over the top of the jam in each jar. You should have a layer that's about an eighth of an inch thick. Make sure it reaches to the edges and touches the glass. Then put the lids on and there you are. Your Own Homemade Strawberry Jam.

NOTE ONE: Don't forget to paste labels on your jam jars. You can buy them and print your name and the kind of jam and the date you made it. If you're planning to give a jar of jam away as a present (and it's a very nice present), you may want to design an extra special label.

NOTE TWO: You can use this recipe to make raspberry and blackberry jam, too.

NOTE THREE: Don't try to make more than four or five jars of jam at a time. You lose the really fresh fruit flavor.

FIVE

A BAKER'S DOZEN
of
WINTER WARMERS
and
TREATS

Winter is the coziest time of all. It's a time for popping good things in the oven, for spicy smells, for hearty food. It's a time for building snowmen and igloos and coming in—all rosy-cheeked—for enormous mugs of hot chocolate. It's a time for friends, for talking and laughing while the snow comes down outside and you're snug in the kitchen pulling taffy. It's a time to welcome father with the smell of freshly baked gingerbread when he comes home through the February slush. It's a time to gather around the fire and be glad that you are you.

BOILAWAY BEEF

This got its name when Jimmy was in bed with a bad cold. His mother gave him a bowlful of steaming hot beef broth with big chunks of boiled beef in it. The next day Jimmy felt much better and he said, "That just boiled away my cold."

You'll need:

> 3 to 4 pounds of brisket of beef (ASK YOUR MOTHER TO HELP YOU CUT OFF MOST OF THE FAT BEFORE YOU START COOKING.)
> 6 leeks
> 1 onion
> 2 cloves
> 8 carrots
> 2 or 3 stalks of celery with the leaves on
> 10 or 12 peppercorns
> 2 teaspoons of salt
> 1 bay leaf
> 1 teaspoon of thyme
> 12 small white onions

1. Put the beef in a large kettle and cover it with cold water.

2. Wash the leeks carefully. Then cut 2 in half the long way. CAREFUL WITH THAT KNIFE! They're pretty aren't they? Wash them again (it's awfully hard to get leeks clean) and put them in the kettle with the beef.

3. Scrape 2 of the carrots with a swivel-blade peeler, cut off the tops and bottoms and throw them away. Cut the rest of the 2 carrots into big pieces and add them to the kettle. Incidentally, I'm hoping you remembered about washing your hands.

4. Peel the onion and stick the cloves in it. Add the onion to the kettle.

5. Wash the celery and put that in.

6. Add the peppercorns, salt, bay leaf and thyme and

put the kettle on the stove. When the water boils, turn the heat way down and put the cover on. Let everything simmer for about 3 hours.

7. While the meat is cooking, wash and split the rest of the leeks and scrape the rest of the carrots. Peel the white onions. I hope they don't make you cry too much.

8. ASK YOUR MOTHER TO CHECK THE MEAT AFTER TWO HOURS AND THEN AFTER TWO AND A HALF HOURS. IT SHOULD BE TENDER, BUT NOT SO TENDER THAT IT WILL FALL APART. WHEN YOUR MOTHER THINKS THE MEAT IS READY, ASK HER TO HELP YOU TAKE IT OUT OF THE KETTLE AND PLACE IT ON A LARGE DISH. THEN STRAIN THE BROTH. BE CAREFUL. IT'S VERY HOT.

9. Rinse out the kettle and put the meat back in. Add the strained broth. And start it simmering again. Add the rest of the vegetables.

10. Let it cook for another half-hour. You can serve it as soon as the vegetables are done. But be sure to taste it (DON'T BURN YOUR TONGUE) to see if it needs more salt or pepper.

NOTE ONE: You can make this ahead of time, even the day before, and warm it up just before dinner time. I think it tastes even better warmed up.

NOTE TWO: You can eat this just as it is. Serve it in a big soup plate. Or put the broth in a soup cup and serve it as a first course and arrange the beef and the vegetables on a platter for the main course.

NOTE THREE: We always serve Boilaway Beef with a sauce or two. The next two recipes are our favorite sauces. See how you like them.

PICKLED BUDDY SAUCE

Does that sound odd to you? The flavor in this sauce comes from capers. Do you know what capers are? They're little pickled flower buds.

You'll need:

    2 tablespoons of butter
    2 tablespoons of flour
    1 cup of hot beef broth from your boiled beef
    2 or 3 tablespoons of capers

1. Remember, I told you earlier that once you learned to make cream sauce, you had learned a technique for making lots of recipes. This is one of them. Turn back to the directions for a cream sauce in the Glop on Toast recipe (it's on page 48) and make a sauce using the butter, flour and beef broth according to those instructions.

2. When the sauce is thick and smooth, just stir in the capers. It's ready to serve.

HOT AND COLD SAUCE

This sauce is served cold, but it has a hot taste. The heat comes from the horseradish in it. This is very easy to make. You simply stir everything together.

You'll need:

    1 small carton of sour cream
    2 tablespoons of chopped parsley
    2 or 3 tablespoons of prepared horseradish.

1. Mix the sour cream, parsley and horseradish together.

2. Taste. If you think you'd like it hotter, add more horseradish.

HISTORICAL BEANS

Boston is known as Beantown. And with good reason. The early settlers used to eat a lot of baked beans. Those New Englanders knew how to keep warm with hearty food during the long cold winters. Most people eat baked beans that come in cans these days. But home-baked beans taste much better.

In Boston, it's a tradition to have baked beans on Saturday night. That means starting to get ready on Friday. You'll need:

2 cups of dried pea beans
¼ pound of salt pork
1 onion
1 teaspoon of salt
1 teaspoon of dry mustard
2 tablespoons of brown sugar
½ cup of molasses

On Friday, here's what you do:
1. Pick through the beans and throw out any that are brown or split. Sometimes little stones get packed in with the beans. So watch out for those, too.
2. Put the beans in a colander and run cold water over them. Shake them around until they're well washed, then put them in a big bowl and cover them with water. Leave them that way overnight.
3. Cut the salt pork into 3 or 4 pieces and put them in a small bowl of cold water to spend the night.

On Saturday morning, here's what you do:

1. Drain the beans and put them in a pan. Cover them with cold water and cook them for about half an hour—until they are *almost* tender. Then drain them again. Pour more cold water over them and drain once more.

2. If your mother has an old-fashioned beanpot, that's the thing to use. Otherwise use a two-quart casserole, one that has a close-fitting cover.

3. Peel the onion. Doesn't it seem as if cooking is just peeling one onion after another? Put the onion in the beanpot, then add half the beans.

4. Push 2 pieces of the salt pork into the beans.

5. Now add the rest of the beans and push the rest of the salt pork into them.

6. Boil 2 cups of water and add the salt, dry mustard, brown sugar and molasses to the boiling water. Stir it around and then pour it over the beans.

7. Cover the beanpot and put it into a 250-degree oven. That's all you have to do for the next 4 hours. This is a good time to clean your room.

8. Take a look at the beans every hour or so. If you don't see a little water bubbling on the top, boil some water and pour it in, just enough to cover the beans.

9. After 4 hours, take the cover off and let the beans keep on cooking another 45 minutes. That's all there is to it.

NOTE: Baked beans are particularly good with frankfurters and homemade johnnycake. Everyone knows how to cook frankfurters, and the recipe for johnnycake is on page 127.

WILD WEST BEANS

Chili is to Texas and the Southwest what baked beans are to Boston and New England—a native dish. And here's a native-tested recipe.

You'll need:

>   2 tablespoons of salad oil
>   1 large onion or 2 small ones
>   ½ a green pepper
>   1 pound of ground beef
>   ½ cup of hot water
>   1½ cups of canned tomatoes
>   2 tablespoons of chili powder
>   2 tablespoons of cold water
>   ½ teaspoon of salt
>   1 teaspoon of sugar
>   1 clove of garlic
>   2 cups of canned kidney beans

1. Get out that big black frying pan again and measure the oil into it.

2. Peel and slice the onion. Fairly thin slices, please. AND BE CAREFUL.

3. Wash the green pepper. (You might as well wash your hands while you're at it.) Scrape off any white membrane and seeds on the inside and cut the half a pepper into small squares.

4. Put the onion and pepper into the frying pan and cook until they are a little soft. Then add the ground beef.

Stir it around and let it cook until the red disappears and it starts to get brown.

5. Now add the hot water and the canned tomatoes.

6. Mix the chili powder with the 2 tablespoons of cold water. Stir it until it's smooth and then add it to the meat.

7. Add the salt and sugar.

8. Peel the garlic clove and chop it up finely. WATCH YOUR FINGERS. It's easiest if you slice it thin first and then chop the slices. Add the garlic to the meat and cover the frying pan. Let the whole thing cook very slowly for an hour. Then take the cover off and cook for another 15 minutes.

9. If it seems too thick, add a little more hot water. Then add the 2 cups of kidney beans. Stir to mix them up with the meat but be gentle. Try not to mash them. Cook the chili about 15 or 20 minutes more. Keep the heat low and stir it occasionally so it won't burn or stick to the pan.

NOTE: Chili is usually served in a soup bowl. Salty crackers and a salad go with it very well. Another good way to serve it is over split pieces of johnnycake. And that's the recipe that's coming up next.

JOHNNYCAKE

This is another recipe from the early days of this country. The pioneers used to call it journey cake. It goes with baked beans and chili the way chocolate sauce goes with vanilla ice cream.

You'll need:

1 cup of yellow cornmeal
1 cup of flour
⅓ cup of sugar
3 teaspoons of baking powder
½ teaspoon of salt
1 egg
1 cup of milk
3 tablespoons of salad oil or melted butter

1. Heat the oven to 425 degrees.
2. Butter an 8-inch-square pan.
3. Put the cornmeal into a mixing bowl.
4. Measure the flour, sugar, baking powder and salt into a flour sifter and sift it over the cornmeal.
5. Beat the egg in a small bowl and add the milk to it. Beat again for just a second to mix the egg and milk. Then pour it over the cornmeal and flour. Add the oil or butter. Mix the whole thing together with your trusty wooden spoon.
6. Pour the batter into the buttered pan (use your rubber spatula to get every last bit out of the mixing bowl) and pop the pan in the oven.
7. Let it bake for 20 minutes. Serve it hot.
NOTE: This is awfully good for breakfast, too. If you have any left over, toast it and spread it with jam the next morning.

THIRD-GENERATION LASAGNE

This Italian dish has become an all-American favorite. My friend Maria was just nine when her mother, who was born in Italy, taught her how to make it. Today, Maria has two sons. They're twins and twelve years old. They have learned to make lasagne so well that Maria tells me it's as good as hers.

You'll need:

    1 onion
    1 tablespoon of olive or salad oil
    1 pound of chopped beef
    1 clove of garlic
    ½ teaspoon of salt
    ½ teaspoon of pepper (And what kind of pepper? Home-ground pepper.)
    ½ teaspoon of oregano
    3 tablespoons of chopped parsley
    2½ cups of stewed tomatoes
    1 can of tomato sauce (the 8-ounce size)
    1 pound of lasagne
    ½ pound of mozzarella cheese, sliced thin
    1½ cups of ricotta or cottage cheese
    Grated Parmesan cheese

1. You can make part of this in the morning and then finish it just before supper. Peel the onion and chop it finely. IF YOU HAVE REACHED THIS FAR IN THIS BOOK WITHOUT CHOPPING AN ONION, PLEASE ASK YOUR MOTHER TO SHOW YOU THE EASIEST AND SAFEST WAY. BUT DON'T EXPECT HER TO DO IT ALL FOR YOU.

2. Put the olive oil in the big black frying pan. Add the chopped onion and cook it until it is soft. Then add the chopped beef. Push the meat around with a cooking fork or spoon to break it up. Cook it until the red disappears.

3. Peel the garlic clove and slice it very thin. Add the garlic, salt, pepper, oregano, parsley, stewed tomatoes and tomato sauce to the meat. Stir it all around and let it simmer (you know, that means just tiny bubbles, not boiling) for half an hour. Then you can put the whole thing

in the refrigerator in a covered dish to wait until you're ready to start cooking supper.

4. About an hour before supper time, cook the lasagne. Just follow the directions on the package. Drain it. BE CAREFUL. ASK YOUR MOTHER TO HELP YOU.

5. Now get out your serving dish. Some people use a rectangular casserole. You can use a large cake pan. ASK YOUR MOTHER WHAT SHE SUGGESTS. Put one-third of the meat sauce that you cooked earlier in the bottom of your serving dish.

6. Then put half the lasagne on top of the meat sauce. Put half the mozzarella slices on top of the lasagne. Put half the ricotta on top of the mozzarella.

7. Now start again with one-third of the meat sauce and the rest of the lasagne, mozzarella, and ricotta. Finish it off with the rest of the meat sauce.

8. Put it in a 350-degree oven for half an hour. Five minutes before it's done, sprinkle grated Parmesan cheese over the top and put it back in the oven until the cheese is toasty golden.

9. That's all there is to it.

SPICY GINGERBREAD

Warm and spicy, there's nothing better to smell than gingerbread baking on a frosty winter afternoon.
You'll need:

> ½ cup of butter
> 1 cup of molasses
> 1 cup of hot water
> 1 egg
> ½ cup of sugar
> 2½ cups of flour
> 1½ teaspoons of baking powder

    ½ teaspoon of salt
    1 teaspoon of cinnamon
    1 teaspoon of mace
    1 teaspoon of ginger

1. Turn the oven on. Set it at 350 degrees.

2. Butter a 9-inch-square pan.

3. Put the butter and molasses and water into a pan. Heat it over low heat until the butter melts.

4. Beat the egg in a small bowl and then pour the sugar over it and beat it some more.

5. Before you measure the flour, put about 3 cups of flour in a sifter, sift it and then measure 2½ cups of the sifted flour. (Don't pack the flour down. The idea of sifting it is to get it light and airy.)

6. Now put the 2½ cups of flour back in the sifter and add the baking powder, salt, cinnamon, mace and ginger.

7. Pour the molasses mixture into a big bowl. Let it cool a little and then sift some of the flour mixture into it and stir. Now add half of the egg and sugar and stir some more. Now sift in more flour and spices. Stir. Add the rest of the egg and sugar. Stir. Sift in the rest of the flour and spices. And now what do you do? That's right, stir some more until it's all well mixed up.

8. Pour it into the buttered pan. Use a rubber spatula to scrape the bowl, so you'll get every bit of batter. Bake it for 50 to 60 minutes. The gingerbread will pull away from the edge of the pan just a smidgen when it's done. And it will feel firm when you poke it (gently, now) with your finger. It takes experience to know when a cake is done. SO ASK YOUR MOTHER.

NOTE ONE: Serve this with whipped cream (the recipe is on the next page) or applesauce. If you want, you

can let it cool and frost it. Look up a plain white frosting
recipe in one of your mother's cookbooks.

NOTE TWO: If there's any gingerbread left, pack a
piece in your school lunch box along with an apple.
That's a dessert fit for an A student.

WHIPPED CREAM

A lot of people just don't seem to know how to whip
cream properly. So here's the basic recipe.
You need:

> 1 cup of heavy cream (It should be 24 hours
>   old. If you get it from the supermarket,
>   don't worry. It's sure to be at least that
>   old.)
> ¼ cup confectioners' sugar
> 1 teaspoon of vanilla

1. You can use the electric mixer, but I think an egg
beater is just as easy—and safer. There's less chance of
your overbeating the cream. (If you beat cream too long,
it turns into butter, you know.) Pour the cream in a good-
sized bowl, whip it with the egg beater until it starts to
get a little heavy. Then start sprinkling in the confectioners' sugar a little at a time.

2. When the cream is quite thick and seems to be ready
to stand up when you lift the egg beater, add the vanilla
and just beat enough to get it mixed in.

NOTE ONE: If you have any applesauce in the house,
add a quarter of a cup when you add the confectioners'
sugar. This is very good with gingerbread.

NOTE TWO: Whipped cream is the basis for many

desserts. For instance, strawberries and whipped cream, white grapes and whipped cream, raspberries and whipped cream, sponge cake and jam and whipped cream. Perhaps you can invent a new combination.

APPLE LOLLYPOPS

These are a special kind of treat. They're good for between-meal snacks. They make a different kind of dessert if you're having friends over for lunch or supper. And they make good Christmas presents.

NOTICE TO PARENTS: Apple lollypops are fun to make, but be sure the Junior Cook (or cooks) is very careful. That hot sugar syrup can give a careless cook a nasty burn. Children should not make these without adult supervision.

You'll need:

    3 bright red apples
    3 lollypop sticks
    1 cup of sugar
    1 cup of light corn syrup
    1 bottle of little red cinnamon candies (about
       2 ounces)
    ½ teaspoon of red food coloring
    ½ teaspoon of cinnamon
    A candy thermometer

1. Butter a cooky sheet.

2. Wash and dry the apples. Cut the stems off. Push the lollypop sticks into the stem end.

3. Put the sugar, corn syrup and cinnamon candies in a pan with one cup of water. Heat and stir until the sugar and candies dissolve. Don't let the mixture boil.

4. When the sugar and candy is dissolved, add the red coloring and the cinnamon. Stir.

5. NOW ASK YOUR MOTHER TO SHOW YOU HOW TO USE THE CANDY THERMOMETER. You have to boil the red mixture until the thermometer registers 300 degrees. Don't stir it while you're boiling it.

6. When the thermometer shows 300, take the pan off the heat. Now you have to work fast, but BE CAREFUL. Dip each apple into the pan of syrup and turn it until it is completely coated with the red syrup.

7. Put the apple on the cooky sheet and let it sit for 10 minutes while the syrup turns into a hard candy coating.

PULLY-TUGGY TAFFY

Ask a couple of friends over for a taffy pull some afternoon. It's fun. Taffy makes a good present. You can wrap it up in transparent plastic wrap and put it in brightly colored bags.

NOTE TO PARENTS: Taffy is fun to make, but children should not be allowed to prepare it without adult supervision. It's too easy to get a serious burn. I suggest that Mother prepare the taffy right through Step 4 until she is positive that the Junior Cook is experienced and careful enough to do it alone.

You'll need:

> 1 cup of molasses
> 1 cup of sugar
> 2 teaspoons of cider vinegar
> 2 tablespoons of butter
> ⅛ teaspoon of salt
> ½ teaspoon of baking soda
> A candy thermometer

1. Butter a 12-by-8-inch pan.

2. Measure the molasses, sugar and vinegar into a large saucepan and cook slowly until the candy thermometer registers 260 degrees. Keep stirring as it cooks.

3. When the 260-degree point is reached, take the pan off the stove and add the butter, salt and baking soda. The mixture will foam, but keep stirring until it stops foaming.

4. Pour it into the buttered pan and let it cool.

5. While the candy is cooling, each person should butter a large plate or pie plate. Oh, and all of you, please wash your hands. Then butter your fingertips.

6. When the candy is cool enough to handle, divide it up. Now the fun begins. It's push and pull and tug until the taffy turns tougher than you are.

7. Push your portion into a lump, then using your thumbs and fingertips, pull it out about 12 inches. Then bring the ends together and fold it into a 6-inch piece. Pull it out again and fold it back again. Keep on doing this until it gets harder and harder to do. Boys are good at this, because they seem to have better arm muscles. Keep on pulling and tugging and folding until the taffy gets quite light in color and just about impossible to pull. Then give it one last pull. You should have a strand of taffy that's about three-quarters of an inch thick. Twist it a little, like a rope.

8. Now get the kitchen scissors and a pan of hot water. Dip the scissor blades into the water and cut the taffy rope into pieces about one inch long. Keep dipping the scissors in the hot water. Otherwise, things will get very sticky.

9. I suppose you'll want to eat it now. If you are mak-

ing it for a present, wrap each piece carefully in wax paper or plastic wrap.

SNOW BOWL

Here is a truly wintry treat to make some crispy cold afternoon when it has been snowing hard all day.

This recipe has two parts, an inside part and an outside part.

For the inside part, you need:

    1 pint of heavy cream
    2 teaspoons of vanilla
    ½ cup of confectioners' sugar

1. Put everything in a bowl and beat it with an egg beater for 2 minutes.

2. Put the bowl in the refrigerator.

3. Put on your boots and mittens and whatever you wear to go out in the snow. Get a big spoon. Take the bowl of cream out of the refrigerator. And you're ready for the outside part.

1. Find a pure white patch of newly fallen snow (I'm afraid that this recipe is not for city dwellers. City snow is not clean enough to eat.)

2. Put the cream bowl securely in the snow and put a few large spoonfuls of snow in it. Stir it in thoroughly.

3. Add some more snow. Stir again.

4. Keep spooning snow into the cream and stirring it until you can't put any more in.

5. Leave the bowl in the snow near the door, while you go in and take off your boots and things.

6. Tell everyone that you're ready. Get out the plates and spoons. Then bring in your Snow Bowl and give everyone a generous helping. Some people say snow is better in January; others like February snow. I don't think it matters.

CHOCOLATE SURVIVAL KIT

When you're cold right down to your toes and up to your nose, hot chocolate will warm you up again. And when you're very cold and very tired, hot chocolate will give you energy. I'm sure you can think of lots of times when you'll need to use this Chocolate Survival Kit.
You'll need:

2 squares of unsweetened chocolate
1 cup of water
3 cups of milk
⅓ cup of sugar
⅛ teaspoon of salt
2 teaspoons of vanilla

1. Melt the chocolate over very, very low heat in a heavy pan.
2. Boil the cup of water and add it to the chocolate while it's melting.
3. Scald the 3 cups of milk. WHEN YOU SCALD MILK, YOU HEAT IT UNTIL LITTLE BUBBLES APPEAR AROUND THE EDGE. CHECK WITH YOUR MOTHER IF YOU'RE NOT SURE.
4. When the milk is scalded, take it off the stove, add the sugar, salt and vanilla. Stir it around and put it aside for a minute.

5. When the chocolate is all melted, turn up the heat so that the mixture will boil. The minute it boils, take it off the heat and pour the hot milk mixture into it.

6. Get out your trusty egg beater and beat the chocolate for half a minute. That's all there is to it.

NOTE: This is good to make when you have friends over. For company, you might like to serve it with a generous dab of whipped cream on top. That's really good.

HAPPY DAYS AND HOLIDAYS

SIX

A BAKER'S DOZEN
of
CELEBRATIONS

Every family has dozens of days to celebrate—birthdays, anniversaries, last day of school (and the first day of school, too), a good report card, a new job for Daddy and Hallowe'en and Christmas and Valentine's Day and Lincoln's and Washington's birthdays and bar mitzvahs and graduations and Thanksgiving and Chanukah and . . .

How many happy days and holidays does your family celebrate?

Sometimes just giving a friend a present turns an ordinary day into a happy day. So when you cook your way through this chapter, you'll be making and sharing happiness.

ONCE-UPON-A-BIRTHDAY CAKE

Of all the happy times, birthdays may be the happiest. And what would a birthday be without a birthday cake and its candles? This cake is in two layers and it really looks impressive.

You'll need:

    1 cup of cake flour (It's very important to sift
        the flour before you measure it. That's
        because sifting lets air get between the
        tiny flour particles. So put a heaping cup
        of flour into the sifter and sift it. Then
        with a big spoon or scoop, fill the measur-
        ing cup. Don't pack the flour down. You
        see how much more flour you seem to
        have? Put the extra back into the flour
        container.)
1½ teaspoons of baking powder
 ¼ teaspoon of salt
 4 eggs
 1 cup of sugar
1½ tablespoons of cold water
1½ tablespoons of fresh lemon juice
 1 teaspoon of vanilla

1. Get out two round 8-inch layer-cake pans. Butter
them very carefully. Make sure that you don't miss any
spots. You don't want your birthday cake to stick to the
pan. Then drop a couple of tablespoons of flour into each
pan and shake the pans back and forth until all the buttered surfaces are dusted with flour. Then turn the pans
upside down over the sink and let the extra flour fall
out.

2. Turn the oven on to 350 degrees.

3. Measure the sifted cup of flour, the baking powder
and the salt into the flour sifter.

4. Break the eggs (CAREFUL NOW, YOU'VE HAD A
LOT OF EXPERIENCE IN BREAKING EGGS IF YOU
STARTED COOKING RIGHT AT THE BEGINNING
OF THIS BOOK, BUT IT'S ALWAYS A DELICATE
OPERATION) and separate the yolks and whites. The

whites should go into a pretty big bowl and the yolks into a smaller bowl.

5. Now it's time to let the electric mixer do some work for you. IF THIS IS THE FIRST TIME YOU'VE USED THE ELECTRIC MIXER, ASK YOUR MOTHER TO TELL YOU HOW TO RUN IT. THE RULE OF THIS COOKALONG BOOK IS THAT NO JUNIOR COOK SHOULD USE THE ELECTRIC MIXER UNLESS A PARENT IS ON HAND. THAT'S FOR SAFETY'S SAKE. WHEN YOUR MOTHER OR FATHER THINKS YOU'RE READY TO SOLO ON THE MIXER, THEY'LL GIVE YOU PERMISSION. OKAY? Beat the whites until they stand up like soft snowdrifts or snow-capped mountains. If you don't have an electric mixer the egg beater is every bit as good. It just takes a little more time and energy.

6. When the egg whites form little peaks, like fluffy snow mountains, beat in a quarter of a cup of the sugar.

7. Now, take the egg white bowl off the mixing stand and put the egg yolk bowl in its place. Don't even bother to wash the beaters. Just start beating the yolks until they get a little thick and are a pale yellow, sort of a lemony color.

8. When the yolks look lemony, add the water and lemon juice and vanilla and the rest of the sugar. Beat the mixture a little longer and then pour it over the beaten egg whites.

9. Now you have to fold the yellow mixture into the white mixture. Folding is like stirring and beating, but it's different. ASK YOUR MOTHER TO SEE THAT YOU DO IT CORRECTLY. Here's the way to do it: Take the rubber spatula that you use to scrape out bowls with and cut right down through the middle of the batter until you

touch the bottom of the bowl. Then scrape the spatula along the bottom of the bowl and up the side. Fold the batter that came up over the top of the mixture. Then repeat. Keep on doing this until the egg whites are pretty well mixed into the yolk mixture. The reason for this folding motion is that you want to get the egg whites mixed in with the yolks without losing the air that you just finished beating into the egg whites. If you were to try to beat them into the yolks, you would force out all that air. And then you would have a very heavy cake. Who wants that? Nobody.

10. Now sift the flour and baking powder and salt over the egg mixture.

11. Fold the flour into the egg mixture. Just use the same spatula and the same motion until the flour is nicely mixed in.

12. Pour your batter into the two cake pans that you buttered and floured and tuck them in the oven.

13. Your cake layers will be done in about 25 to 30 minutes. Here's how you tell for sure whether they're done. When 25 minutes is up, open the oven door gently and press your finger down softly on the top of one of the cakes. If the cake springs back, it's done. If not, let it bake another 5 minutes. I SUGGEST YOU ASK YOUR MOTHER TO MAKE THE FINGER TEST ALONG WITH YOU. AS THEY SAY, "IT'S BETTER TO BE SAFE THAN SORRY." Right?

14. Now take two thick pot holders and take your cake pans out of the oven, one at a time. Turn them upside down on a wire rack and leave them alone until they are cool. Then run a metal spatula around the edge—gently, now—and just help them out of the pans. IF YOU'RE

HAVING TROUBLE, ASK THE NEAREST PARENT FOR SOME HELP.

15. Now your birthday cake is ready for frosting. ASK YOUR MOTHER TO HELP YOU CHOOSE A FROSTING RECIPE FROM ONE OF HER COOKBOOKS.

CRANKY ICE CREAM

Ice cream just isn't what it used to be. Not if you buy it at the store. Most store-bought ice cream is artificially flavored and full of neutralizers, buffers, bactericides, stabilizers, emulsifiers and antoxidants. Yecch! When you make your own, you can be sure that there are no chemicals in it—just the very best cream and eggs and sugar.

Making ice cream is truly a family affair. This is called Cranky Ice Cream because it's made in an old-fashioned freezer that has to be cranked by hand. There are electric freezers, but somehow the ice cream doesn't taste quite as good—and it's not half as much fun to make.

So, the first thing you need is an old-fashioned freezer.* You can still buy them because there are still people who insist on good food made with good ingredients, not with chemicals and artificial flavors. I hope you're one of them.

---

* Mother, please don't groan. They're not so expensive, considering they're a lifetime investment. If you can't find one at your local hardware store, Sears, Roebuck has them for about $16. You can also get them with your Green Stamps and other trading stamps.

You'll need:

    1½ cups of light cream
    ⅔ cup of sugar
    ¼ teaspoon of salt
    4 egg yolks (To use up the egg whites there's
        a recipe for Meringues and one for Seedy
        Cookies in the Junior Gourmet chapter.)
    1½ tablespoons of vanilla
    2 cups of heavy cream

(Ice cream is sometimes called frozen custard. And there's a good reason for that. It's exactly what it is. When you learn how to make custard, you've learned how to make one more sauce that is important in cooking. And it's not just for desserts. When you get to the Junior Gourmet chapter, you'll find a recipe for onion and cheese pie that uses a custard sauce.)

1. Get out the double boiler. Put some water in the bottom, but be sure that it won't touch the top of the double boiler when you fit the top on. IT'S IMPORTANT TO MAKE SURE THAT YOU DON'T PUT TOO MUCH WATER IN. IF YOU DO, YOU WILL CURDLE YOUR CUSTARD!

2. Pour the light cream into the top of the double boiler and heat it over the water until there's a little film on the top. DO NOT LET THE CREAM BOIL.

3. When you see the film, stir in the sugar and salt. When the sugar is dissolved, take the top part of the double boiler out and put it aside to cool slightly.

4. Put the egg yolks in a medium-sized bowl and beat them just a little with an egg beater or a wire whisk. NOW ASK YOUR MOTHER TO PLEASE COME HELP YOU. THE NEXT STEP IS CRUCIAL.

5. Once the egg yolks are beaten, you need to pour

some of the hot cream and sugar into them. BUT YOU HAVE TO BE VERY CAREFUL. IF YOU POUR TOO MUCH OF THE HOT CREAM IN AT ONCE, YOU'LL COOK THE EGG YOLKS. SO YOU HAVE TO POUR IT IN JUST A TINY BIT AT A TIME AND STIR THE EGG YOLKS LIKE MAD WHILE YOU'RE DOING IT. I SUGGEST THAT THE SENIOR COOK DO THE POURING AND THE JUNIOR COOK DO THE STIR-RING.

6. Keep pouring the hot cream into the egg yolks and stirring furiously until you've used up about a cup of the cream, then pour the egg yolk-and-cream mixture into the remaining cream in the top of the double boiler. And keep stirring.

7. Put the top of the double boiler back on the bottom part. The water in the bottom should be simmering. Keep on stirring it until it gets smooth and creamy—sort of like a light mayonnaise. When the custard leaves a film on the stirring spoon, it's done. But don't get impatient. It takes a good 15 minutes, sometimes more. When it's done, take it off the heat, pour it into a large bowl, and let it cool.

8. When the custard is completely cool, stir in the va-nilla and the 2 cups of heavy cream. And that's it—as far as the cooking goes.

9.. Freeze it. All you have to do is follow the directions that came with your hand-cranked freezer. Since hand-cranked ice cream is a family affair, father or mother should take over at this point and discuss the freezer in-structions with the Junior Cook. But just in case you don't have the instructions, here are the basics.

HOW TO FREEZE CRANKY ICE CREAM

1. Pour your vanilla custard into the ice cream freezer can and insert the dasher. Close the can tightly.

2. Fit the can into the freezer tub and then pack crushed ice and rock salt all around it. Use eight parts of crushed ice to one part of rock salt.

3. Let the can stand in the salt and ice for 5 minutes and then begin cranking. The secret is to start turning the crank very slowly until you begin to feel a little bit of resistance, then you should turn it faster. The experts tell me that this is the way to get the best flavor and texture. Keep turning until it becomes just about impossible. This is why it's a family affair. You need plenty of muscle for this. It's a good idea to take turns.

4. When it's just too difficult to turn, the ice cream is done. BUT DON'T EAT IT YET. Store it in your refrigerator freezer for 2 hours. This makes the flavor better. People say it "mellows" or "seasons" it. But you get a chance to sample. When you pull the dasher out before you put the finished ice cream in the freezer, you can lick the dasher.

NOTE ONE: If you prefer chocolate ice cream, add 2 squares of bitter chocolate to the light cream when you scald it.

NOTE TWO: If you like peppermint stick ice cream, crack up a half pound of peppermint sticks and stir them into the ice cream just when it gets halfway difficult to crank. BE CAREFUL, WHEN YOU TAKE THE ICE CREAM CAN OUT OF THE FREEZER TO MIX IN THE PEPPERMINT CANDY, WIPE OFF THE CAN

AND COVER SO THAT THE SALT AND WATER
DON'T GET INTO THE ICE CREAM.

CHANUKAH SEEDY COOKIES

Chanukah is one of the happiest Jewish holidays. Children like it because it lasts for eight days and the custom
is for parents to give their children a present on every
single night of the Chanukah festival. These cookies are
often served for dessert at one of the eight holiday dinners. And it might be a nice idea to make them as a
present for your parents. They were children once, too.
You'll need:

    2 egg whites
    ¼ cup of cake flour
    ½ teaspoon of salt
    1 cup of confectioners' sugar (Sift the sugar
        before you measure it. Then pile the sifted
        sugar into the measuring cup with a large
        spoon or scoop. Do not pack it down.)
    1 cup of sesame seeds

1. Turn the oven on to 400 degrees. Grease a couple of
cooky sheets and get your ingredients together.
2. Beat the egg whites with your egg beater until they
are stiff and stand up like little white mountains.
3. Measure the flour and salt and sifted sugar into the
flour sifter and sift it over your beaten egg whites.
4. Fold the sifted mixture into the egg whites with a
rubber spatula just the way you did when you were making birthday cake. If you don't remember how, turn back

to Once-Upon-a-Birthday Cake. It's on page 141. And Step 9 tells you how to fold.

5. When the dry things are pretty well mixed with the egg whites, start adding the sesame seeds a spoonful or two at a time. Fold them in gently with your rubber spatula.

6. Now take a teaspoon and drop your cooky batter in tidy rows—not too close together—on the cooky sheets.

7. Bake them for just 10 minutes. Use a metal spatula to take them off the cooky sheets and let them cool on a metal rack.

8. Happy Chanukah!

CHRISTMAS IS DELICIOUS

Decorations Good Enough to Eat

Part of the fun of Christmas is decorating the tree and the house. And when you can eat the decorations, well, that's sort of an extra Christmas present.

POPCORN BALLS

These are fun to make. And the whole family can make them together. In fact, the more hands the merrier.
You'll need:

> 1½ cups of popcorn kernels
> 1 cup of light molasses
> 1 cup of light corn syrup
> 1 tablespoon of vinegar
> 3 tablespoons of butter
> ½ teaspoon of salt
>   A candy thermometer is helpful.

NOTE TO PARENTS: Popping corn and making candy are a lot of fun for both Junior and Senior Cooks. It's important to remember that both can be DANGEROUS. The high temperatures of the candy syrup and the obvious dangers of the open fire or the electric corn popper make this a recipe that requires adult cooperation.

1. Pop your corn. The way that's the most fun is to shake it in an old-fashioned wire corn popper over the hot coals in the fireplace. If you don't have a fireplace, follow the instructions that came with your electric corn popper. And if you don't have an electric corn popper, here's what you do: Choose a heavy pan or skillet that has a cover that fits tightly. Melt 1 tablespoon of butter in the pan, then add ½ cup of popcorn. Put on the cover. And cook it over medium heat on the stove, shaking it back and forth all the time. You'll hear the corn start to pop. When it stops popping, take the pan off the heat and pour the popped corn out into a large bowl. Pick out any hard kernels that didn't pop and throw them away. Then pop another half cup of popcorn kernels. And another.

2. Pour the molasses, the corn syrup and the vinegar into a pan. Attach the candy thermometer to the side of the pan and cook the mixture. Stir it every once in a while until the thermometer reaches 270 degrees.

3. Now take the pan off the heat and stir in the butter and the salt.

4. Pour the molasses mixture over the popcorn in the large bowl. Use a wooden spoon and stir the popcorn around so that it all gets coated.

5. Butter your hands (wash them first, of course) and pick up a big handful of popcorn. Pat it into a popcorn ball and set it on a piece of wax paper or aluminum foil to harden. This will make about 15 to 20 popcorn balls.

6. When the balls are hard and cold, it's time to wrap them.

GOOD IDEA ONE: Wrap each popcorn ball in transparent colored paper. Twist the paper together at the top and then tie a silver or gold string about the twist to keep the paper together. Leave the string long enough so that you can tie the balls to the Christmas tree.

GOOD IDEA TWO: Wrap the balls in transparent colored paper and arrange them on a large platter in the middle of the dining table. This makes a very good Christmas centerpiece. You can add little pieces of evergreen or holly if you like.

GINGERBREAD MEN AND WOMEN AND STARS AND WREATHS, ET CETERA

These cookies can be cut out to make Gingerbread Men and Women, Christmas Stars and Wreaths and Trees and Santa Clauses and Reindeers, all sorts of shapes. You can decorate them with frosting and raisins and nuts and currants and little candies. They make wonderful ornaments to hang on the Christmas tree. (Whenever you're hungry, you can just reach up and pick a Christmas Tree cooky.) And they make delicious presents.

You'll need:

        ¾ cup of molasses
        ¾ cup of butter or margarine
        ¾ cup of brown sugar
       4½ cups of flour
        1 teaspoon of baking powder
        1 teaspoon of salt
        ½ teaspoon of soda
        2 teaspoons of ginger

2 teaspoons of cinnamon
1 teaspoon of cloves
1 egg
1 tablespoon of fresh grated orange rind

1. Before you start cooking, it's a good idea to decide what kind of shapes you want. Maybe you should make a special trip to the store and pick out some special Christmas cooky cutters. I think the Gingerbread Men and Women are the most fun to decorate. But Christmas Tree shapes are fun, too. And so are Wreaths. In fact, it gets very hard to make up one's mind.

2. Heat the molasses in a pretty big pan until you see little bubbles around the edge, then take it off the stove and add the butter to it. Stir it all around until the butter melts. Then put the brown sugar in and stir that all around. Now, put this aside and . . .

3. Measure all these things into a flour sifter—the flour, the baking powder, the salt, the soda, the ginger and the cinnamon, the cloves.

4. Break the egg into a little bowl and beat it just a little. You can use an egg beater if you want, but a fork is just as easy.

5. See if the molasses mixture is cool. If it is, sift all the things in the flour sifter into the molasses mixture. Then add the beaten egg to it. Then add the grated orange rind.

6. Mix it all up very well. It will get stiff, but you keep stirring until everything is well mixed.

7. Now, tear off a big piece of wax paper or aluminum foil and put the cooky mixture in it. Wrap it up very well so no air will get at it and put it in the refrigerator for 2 hours.

8. This is a good time to do some homework or help your mother for 2 hours.

9. Now, wash your hands again. (You washed them before you started, didn't you?) Turn the oven to 350 degrees and ASK YOUR MOTHER TO COME HELP YOU. It's time to roll out the cookies. Put a little flour on a pastry board or you can put it straight on the kitchen table if the table is covered with Formica. ASK YOUR MOTHER. Then take the rolling pin and roll out the cooky dough so that it's about one quarter of an inch thick. If the dough gets too sticky, put it back in the refrigerator for a while, then start again.

10. Is it all rolled out nicely? Okay, now you take the cooky cutter and cut out as many as you can. You'll have some dough left over, but you can squeeze it together and roll it out again.

11. Now, if you plan to use the cookies to hang on the Christmas tree, make a little hole near the top of each cooky for the string to go through. Don't make it too close to the edge. ASK YOUR MOTHER TO SHOW YOU HOW FAR AWAY FROM THE EDGE TO MAKE THE HOLE. What do you make the hole with? Well, you can just use the tip of a sharp kitchen knife or a nail or the tip of your swivel blade peeler. ASK YOUR MOTHER FOR SUGGESTIONS.

12. Put the cookies—you can use a spatula to lift them up—on a buttered cooky sheet and bake them in the oven for 12 minutes.

13. Take them out and let them cool on a cake rack. DON'T EAT THEM YET. The fun part is coming. Oh well, if you want to, go ahead. Eat one or two—just to test them. Pretty good, huh?

14. Now, let's get busy and make some frosting to decorate them. Or you can wait until tomorrow if you've had enough cooking today.

You'll need:

¼ cup of hot water
Confectioners' sugar
1 teaspoon of vanilla

1. Pour the hot water into a bowl. Then add confectioners' sugar, a few spoonfuls at a time.

2. Keep stirring the sugar in until your frosting seems thick enough to spread. Then add the vanilla.

3. If you have an electric mixer, turn it on medium and beat the frosting for about 2 minutes. If it seems a little bit runny, add a spoon or two more of confectioners' sugar and beat it another half a minute. REMEMBER, THE RULE ABOUT THE ELECTRIC MIXER? A GROWN-UP SHOULD BE AROUND WHEN YOU'RE OPERATING IT.

4. If you don't have an electric mixer, it's up to you— your strong wooden spoon, and your strong right arm.

5. Now the fun begins. Take a spatula and start frosting your cookies.

GOOD IDEA ONE: You can divide the frosting into three custard cups and use vegetable coloring (add 1 drop at a time until you get the color you like) to help you in your decorating. For instance, how about white, red and green frosting?

GOOD IDEA TWO: You might want to frost the whole cooky in basic white and then add trimmings in red or green. ASK YOUR MOTHER TO SHOW YOU HOW TO FORCE FROSTING THROUGH A PASTRY BAG WITH DECORATING TIPS. You'll have to make your frosting a little stiffer by using more sugar if you want to force it through the pastry bag. But this is a lot of fun. You can experiment with all sorts of things. For instance, frost your wreath-shaped cookies in green and then decorate them with little red dots of frosting to make holly wreaths.

GOOD IDEA THREE: There are other ways to decorate. Once you've frosted your cookies, you can use bits of candied cherries and raisins and currants and those little candy silver balls and red cinnamon drops to make faces and buttons and all kinds of decorations. Just use your imagination and have a good time.

NOTE ONE: You don't have to wait for Christmas to make these cookies. They're good all year round. You can make heart-shaped cookies for Valentine's Day and pumpkin-shaped cookies for Hallowe'en. And you can make your own designs. Here's how. Decide on your design. Suppose you want to make a cat cooky. Draw the design on a piece of stiff cardboard and then cut it out very carefully. Place the cardboard on your rolled-out cooky dough and cut out the cat with a sharp knife. Use your imagination.

TASTY PRESENTS

FOR FRIENDS AND RELATIVES
FOR BIRTHDAY AND HOSTESS AND THANK-YOU AND
CHRISTMAS AND SURPRISE GIFTS
FOR JUST-BECAUSE-I-LIKE-YOU PRESENTS

There are all sorts of times when you want to give presents. And most young people don't have much money to spend. Fortunately, the most welcome gift of all is something you make yourself. It shows that you care enough about the person to spend time and thought. And that's much more important than money. The next three recipes make excellent presents. They look good and they taste the same way. I hope you'll have a lot of fun making them for people you really like.

GREEN CHEESE BALLS

People used to say that the moon was made of green cheese. Maybe they weren't so far off. The astronauts found some green rocks up there, which surprised them very much. These Green Cheese Balls are a very good present for grown-ups—for Christmas or New Year's or a birthday or an anniversary. They are an excellent addition to the cocktail tray. Everyone will exclaim about how handsome they look and how good they taste. You can make a cheese ball a day or two or three before you plan to give it. Then add the finishing touches just before wrapping it up.

You'll need:

½ to ⅓ of a pound of blue cheese
3 jars of blue-cheese spread (Get the 5-ounce size)
2 tablespoons of sour cream
1 tablespoon of minced celery ("Minced" means that it should be cut in extremely small pieces.)
3 scallions
1 large bunch of parsley
      OR
1 cup of very finely chopped walnuts
    (If you have an electric mixer, making a cheese ball is practically no work at all. Even if you have to mix it by hand, it's not much work.)

1. One or two or three or four days before you plan to give the cheese ball away, crumble the blue cheese into a big bowl. Add the blue-cheese spread, the sour cream, and the celery.

2. Snip the scallions into little pieces with your kitchen scissors. Use both the white and green part of the scallions and add them to the bowl.

3. If you have a mixer, turn it on to medium speed (AND REMEMBER YOU DON'T USE THE MIXER WITHOUT AN ADULT KEEPING AN EYE ON THINGS UNTIL YOU'VE BEEN CLEARED BY YOUR MOTHER OR FATHER TO SOLO ON THE ELEC-TRIC MIXER.) Just let it go until the mixture is nice and fluffy. Scrape down the sides of the bowl with a rubber or plastic spatula so that everything gets mixed in. (BUT KEEP THE SPATULA AWAY FROM THE BEATERS. OKAY?)

4. If you don't have a mixer, you'll just have to use elbow grease. Mix everything together with a stirring motion and then start beating. You remember, use that down, up and over motion. ASK YOUR MOTHER TO DEMONSTRATE.

5. Cover the bowl very tightly with plastic wrap or with aluminum foil and put it in the refrigerator overnight.

6. In the morning, scrape the cheese out of the bowl onto a big square of aluminum foil. Shape the cheese into a ball and wrap the foil around it carefully. Then wrap it in another layer of foil and put it in the refrigerator. It can stay there for several days.

7. About half an hour before you're ready to wrap the

present, wash the parsley, shake it very dry in a clean dish towel and then snip it with the kitchen scissors or chop it with a sharp knife. WATCH OUT FOR YOUR FINGERS.

8. Now take the cheese ball out of the refrigerator. Unwrap it. If it has lost its shape, pat it back into a ball and then roll it around in the parsley until it's completely coated. That's all there is to it. Now wrap it carefully in plastic wrap. It's ready for its final gift wrapping.

9. If you prefer, you can roll the cheese ball in the chopped walnuts instead of in the parsley.

NOTE: If you're invited to spend the weekend with one of your friends, a cheese ball would be a very thoughtful gift to take along with you for your friend's mother.

PEACHES IN A BASKET

These are really pretty. They look just like peaches and everyone will be very very impressed when you tell them that you baked them. In Austria and Germany it's a tradition to make them at Christmastime. But they make wonderful Valentine presents and birthday presents, too. They're a lot of work, but if you are cooking along with your mother, you can divide up the work and then it will be fun. Be sure to read the recipe all the way through so you can plan your time.

You'll need:

4 eggs

1 cup of milk

1½ cups of peanut oil or corn oil

1 teaspoon of vanilla

2 cups of sugar

1½ teaspoons of baking powder

7½ cups of flour (You may not need quite this much. On the other hand you might need just a little more. You can't tell until you . start stirring it in.)

1 jar of apricot preserves, the 12-ounce size

1 bar of German sweet chocolate, the 4-ounce size

1 cup of chopped walnuts (You can buy walnuts already chopped, but they're not fine enough. You'll have to do more chopping yourself. BE CAREFUL WITH THAT KNIFE.)

Rum (If you don't have any, you can use apricot nectar instead.)

4 egg whites

½ pound red-colored sugar and ¾ pound of yellow-colored sugar (You can usually find this in the supermarket.)

Artificial leaves (You can find sprigs of little artificial leaves in five and tens and any place they sell artificial flowers.)

(YOU HAVE TO MIX THE PEACH BATTER A GOOD TWO HOURS BEFORE YOU START BAKING. AREN'T YOU GLAD YOU READ THIS RECIPE THROUGH?)

So for the first part of the recipe, here's what you do—

1. Break the 4 eggs into a big bowl and beat them until they are a little frothy.

2. Then add the wet things—the milk, the peanut oil,

and the vanilla—to the eggs. Stir them around to mix them.

3. Now add the sugar and the baking powder and beat (YOU REMEMBER HOW TO BEAT? ASK YOUR MOTHER TO SHOW YOU IF YOU'VE FORGOT-TEN.) until everything is well mixed.

4. Now add 6 tablespoons of the flour—1 tablespoon at a time—and beat the mixture after you add each tablespoon so that it's well mixed in. Now set the bowl of batter in some safe place and let it rest for 2 hours.

ALL RIGHT. THE TWO HOURS ARE UP. IT'S TIME TO START THE SECOND PART OF THE REC-IPE. WASH YOUR HANDS AGAIN. TIE ON YOUR APRON. AND LET'S GET TO WORK.

1. Beat in the rest of the flour 1 cup at a time until you have a dough that is soft, but holds together. And it should look smooth.

2. Turn the oven on to 325 degrees.

3. Butter two or three cooky sheets. I know you can probably only put two in the oven at a time, but the more cooky sheets you have, the faster you can bake these cookies.

4. Be sure your hands are very clean. Now pinch off a little piece of the dough. Careful, a gentle pinch. You don't need to hurt it. Shape it into a little ball about the size of a walnut. Put the little balls in tidy rows on the cooky sheets and bake them for about 12 minutes. Don't expect them to get brown. They should be sort of pasty colored.

5. Take the cooky sheets out of the oven. (CAREFUL. BE SURE YOU'RE USING GOOD THICK POT HOLD-ERS.) Let the cookies cool on a wire cake rack.

6. When they're cool, you have to get to work. And be careful. This is delicate work. If there are two of you, it will go faster and be more fun.

7. Here's what you do. Hold the cooky so the flat side is toward you and start scooping out its insides with the point of a knife. Scrape out most of the inside. Try to just leave the shell. And, for heaven's sake, be gentle, it's easy to cut through the shell and you don't want to do that.

8. Save the cooky crumbs. You're going to need them.

NOW IF YOU'RE TIRED YOU CAN STOP WHEN YOU'VE SCOOPED OUT ALL THE COOKIES. IF YOU WANT TO TAKE AN HOUR OFF, THAT WON'T HURT ANYTHING. THE BEST PART IS THE THIRD PART. SO WHEN YOU'RE READY, HERE'S WHAT YOU DO:

1. Melt the chocolate. Put it in a medium-size heat-resistant bowl and put the bowl on the stove in a pan of hot water until the chocolate is melted.

2. When the chocolate is melted, add the apricot preserves, the chopped walnuts and about 3½ cups of the cooky crumbs that you saved. Mix everything up and then add enough rum to make the mixture fairly moist.

3. Using a spoon or your fingers (I use my fingers), fill the hollow cookies with this yummy mixture.

4. Now stick two of the cookies together. You see how they begin to look a little like a peach? Well, the shape does. Not the color yet, of course.

5. When the cookies are all filled and stuck together, beat the four egg whites in a shallow bowl until they are just frothy.

6. Now, pour out the red sugar on a big plate.

7. Pour out the yellow sugar—or part of it—on another big plate.

8. Here comes the big transformation. Roll each peach in the egg white.

9. Then plunk it—lightly now—in the red sugar. Make a couple of small red spots on the cooky.

10. Now, roll your peach in the yellow sugar and put it on the wire rack to dry.

11. Cut off one of the artificial leaves and stick it in the crack between the two cooky halves. Now, doesn't that look really peachy? (Don't bother sticking the leaves in the rest of the peaches until the very end. I just wanted you to see how it would look. It's more efficient to stick the leaves in all at once when you've finished coloring your peaches.)

12. When the peaches are dry, they should be carefully stored in a covered tin unless you're planning to give them as presents.

13. If the peaches are for presents, here's a great way to wrap them. Ask your grocer for some of the small green boxes they pack fruits and vegetables in. They don't cost very much. Then, depending on the size of the box, place half a dozen or more peaches in each box and cover with plastic wrap. Doesn't that look impressive?

14. This recipe will make about 60 peaches, so you'll probably have plenty left over to munch on.

GOOD IDEA: This is a good present to give your teacher.

YOUR OWN PÂTÉ MAISON

In France, many people start their dinner with a slice of a pâté. Almost every French housewife has her own recipe for pâté. And she usually keeps it a secret. A pâté maison is a pâté that's made at home—and just the way you like it. If you pack this into attractive little bowls or tiny crocks, it makes a good present. People will serve it with little crackers at cocktail time. Or as a first course for dinner.

You'll need:

1 pound of liverwurst
1 tablespoon of Worcestershire sauce
2 tablespoons of very finely chopped onion
½ teaspoon of black pepper (And, of course, you'll grind it in your own pepper mill)
2 tablespoons of sherry or red wine or white wine or brandy
6 tablespoons of butter
1 small bunch of parsley
        OR
1 small bottle of pimento-stuffed olives

1. Squeeze the liverwurst out of its skin into a bowl. Scrape the inside of the skin with a spoon to make sure you've got everything out.

2. Put everything else in the bowl except the parsley and the bottle of olives.

3. Turn on the electric mixer (IS THERE A PARENT IN THE KITCHEN?) to medium and let it go until everything is well mixed. Keep pushing down the liverwurst around the edge of the bowl with a rubber spatula.

4. Now pack your pâté into the little bowls or crocks.

5. Sprinkle the top with the chopped parsley or decorate it with olive slices.

6. Wrap your little crocks of pâté very carefully in plastic wrap and put them in the refrigerator until it's present time.

NOTE: You don't absolutely have to give this away. It's good for Sunday night supper. Just spread it on some crusty French bread, and serve it with a green salad. It's a meal fit for a king—or for you.

HOLIDAY BIRD

Roast chicken seems to be just what the doctor ordered for holidays and other happy days. Serve it hot or serve it cold. Serve it stuffed or serve it unstuffed. But serve it. Almost everyone likes it.

You'll need:

    1 4- to 5-pound roasting chicken (Buy one that
        has not been frozen. It will taste better.)
    6 to 8 tablespoons of butter
    2 onions
    5 or 6 sprigs of parsley
    Salt
    Pepper

1. When you unwrap the chicken, rinse it off under cold running water. Then pat it dry with paper towels.

2. Now look your bird over. Are there any tiny hairs on his legs? Or little pinfeathers sticking out of his skin? You certainly don't want those. They don't look very attractive. And they're not what you'd call good eating. CHECK WITH YOUR MOTHER. ASK HER IF SHE HAS A PAIR OF TWEEZERS YOU CAN USE TO PICK OUT THE LITTLE PINFEATHERS. The best way to get rid of those hairy legs is to singe the hair off with a match. BUT CHECK THIS OUT WITH YOUR MOTHER FIRST, PLEASE, BEFORE YOU START LIGHTING MATCHES.

3. Put the giblets that were packed with your chicken in a small pan with a cup and a half of cold water. Peel 1 onion and add that, along with a couple of the sprigs of parsley and ½ teaspoon of salt. Let this simmer for half an hour. Then turn the heat up and let it boil until

about a third of the liquid has boiled away. Take it off the heat. You can use the liquid for basting your chicken.

4. Peel the other onion (BE CAREFUL WITH THAT KNIFE), cut it in quarters and tuck it inside the chicken.

5. Put 2 tablespoons of the butter inside the chicken and the rest of the parsley.

6. Turn the oven on to 400 degrees.

7. Now you need some white string. Take a piece and wrap it around the chicken's ankles. (I suppose chickens don't really have ankles, but you know what I mean.) Pull the string tight and make a knot. Now take a longish piece of string and loop it around the chicken so that it will hold the wing tips close to the body. Make another knot. You need one more long piece of string. Loop this around the chicken again so that it goes around the drumsticks. Tie that knot and you're finished with the string.

8. Take the rest of the butter—it should be fairly soft by now—and rub it all over the chicken. Sprinkle the chicken with salt and pepper from your pepper mill. Pat the salt and pepper into the butter.

9. Place the chicken on a wire rack in a roasting pan on its side. Roast it for 20 minutes.

10. After 20 minutes, turn the chicken on to the other side. Baste it with half the liquid from the giblet pan. Basting just means to spoon the liquid over the chicken carefully. It keeps it moist and tasty.

11. After another 20 minutes, turn the chicken on its back and baste it with the rest of the giblet liquid. Scoop up some of the liquid from the pan and baste the bird with that, too.

12. Let the bird roast another 10 minutes and baste it

again. Now put it back in the oven. In 10 more minutes it should be done.

13. Here's how to test for doneness: Wiggle one of his drumsticks. If it moves easily, the chicken is done. If it doesn't, leave the bird in the oven a few more minutes.

NOTE: This chicken is absolutely delicious. It's as good cold as it is hot. Serve it with a green salad and some crusty French bread and butter for a wonderful gala lunch. If you're having a party buffet, roast two or three chickens depending on the number of people.

FISHERMEN'S PICNIC BASKET

A picnic is certainly a Happy Day event and fishing is fun for everyone—except perhaps the fish. And sometimes the very youngest member of the family turns out to be the one who catches the biggest fish. But there's more to a fishing excursion than fishing. Eating is at least half the fun. This picnic basket will provide good eating for fishermen of all ages whether they're at the lake, beside the trout stream or dangling their lines over the stern of a rowboat, just as long as there's a suitable place to build a campfire later or set up a charcoal grill.

(I'd like to suggest one safety measure—just in case the fish aren't biting. Tuck in some hot dogs or wrap up the makings of Grate Chicken—the recipe's on page 103—so you won't go hungry.)

The easiest way to get a picnic basket together in a hurry is for each picnicker to choose one thing to prepare and get all the ingredients together and wrap them up and put them in the basket. MOTHER SHOULD BE

RESPONSIBLE FOR SEEING THAT PAPER PLATES AND NAPKINS AND FORKS AND KNIVES AREN'T FORGOTTEN.

FIRST CATCH YOUR FISH

Goodness knows what's biting today, but unless it's a whale or a turtle, it should taste pretty good cooked this way.

Pack up:

> Salt and pepper
> 1 sliced lemon (or 2 if you really like lemon
>   a lot)
> Olive oil or salad oil

1. Put all these together in a paper bag and write on it: FISH FIXINGS.
2. Now catch your fish. And then clean him. HERE'S WHERE FATHER IS THE STAR. HE CAN SHOW EVERYONE JUST HOW TO GO ABOUT CLEANING A FISH. And if there's more than one fish, somebody else gets a chance to try his hand at cleaning it.
3. Now with the same knife that you used to clean the fish make little crisscross marks in the skin. This is called scoring.
4. Rub the fish all over with oil.
5. Sprinkle salt and pepper all over it—inside and out.
6. Tuck 1 or 2 lemon slices inside the fish.
7. Put it on the grill. Or hold it over the campfire in one of those hinged wire broilers with a long handle.
8. Cook until done. You have to decide that for yourself. A fish that's about 2 inches thick will be done after it

has cooked 12 minutes on each side. Cut a little piece of it to test. If it's flaky, it's done.

9. Serve the fish with a lemon slice or two for each person. Perhaps you'll want a little more salt and pepper. It should be absolutely delicious.

CAMPFIRE POTATOES

The campfire or the charcoal grill should be started at least an hour before you plan to grill your fish. While you're waiting for the coals to reach the grilling stage, you can start cooking. Start with Campfire Potatoes.

Here's what you do before you leave home. Get together:

> 1 baking potato for each person (Choose big ones and make sure they're all about the same size.)
> Salt
> Pepper (You'll want to have freshly ground pepper, so get out the pepper mill.)
> Butter

1. Wash the potatoes very carefully with a brush. Then slice the potatoes into ¾-inch-wide pieces. Spread each one with butter and then sprinkle it with salt and pepper.

2. Put the slices back together again to re-form the potato and wrap each potato very carefully in aluminum foil. I suggest you use two layers of wrapping. Even three layers wouldn't be too much.

3. Put the potatoes in a bag and label it: CAMPFIRE POTATOES.

4. When the fire is under way, put the wrapped potatoes right under the coals. PLEASE BE CAREFUL. DON'T TAKE CHANCES. YOUR MOTHER OR FATHER SHOULD HELP YOU STICK THESE IN THE FIRE.

5. They'll take about 50 minutes to bake.

6. Serve them in the foil. BE CAREFUL. THEY ARE HOT, HOT, HOT! You may want a little more salt and pepper. Who knows?

ONIONS, HOORAY!

Everyone has a very definite opinion about onions. Some people love them. Other people say, "I love them, but they don't like me." Well, I like onions—and I hope they like me. These onions are perfect for campfire cooking. They're wrapped in foil, just like the potatoes.

Before you leave home, get together:

> 1 or 2 onions for each person (It depends on how
>   well they like onions—or onions like them.)
> Butter
> Salt
> Pepper (you know, freshly ground)
> 1 tablespoon of grated Parmesan cheese for each
>   onion

1. Peel the onions and cut them into ½ -inch thick slices.

2. Tear off a square of aluminum foil for each onion and put 1 sliced onion in the middle of each piece of foil.

3. Put about a tablespoon of butter, some salt and pepper and the grated cheese over the onion slices.

4. Fold the aluminum foil over the onion and its fixings. Then wrap this up in another piece of aluminum foil to make sure that the juice won't run out when it cooks. Put all your onion packages into a bag, mark it ONIONS and pack it in the picnic basket.

5. The onions should cook on the grill. They take about the same time as the potatoes.

FOILED AGAIN CORN

The corn can be cooked at the same time as the fish. I hope your fire is big enough for two cooks to operate without bumping elbows. If it isn't, the fish griller will have to keep an eye on the corn, too.

Before you leave home, get together:

> 2 ears of corn for each person
> Butter
> Salt
> Pepper (freshly ground, please)

1. Husk the corn and be sure to pull out all the little silky threads.

2. Rub butter all over each ear of corn. Be very generous. The more the better.

3. Sprinkle each buttered ear with salt and pepper.

4. Wrap each ear in several thicknesses of aluminum foil. Be sure that it's very securely sealed. Then put all your aluminum foil packages into a bag, mark it CORN, and pack it in the picnic basket.

5. When you're ready, the corn takes about 15 minutes to cook over hot coals. Each piece should be turned at least 4 times so that it will be cooked on all sides.

6. Serve it in its foil. AND WATCH YOUR FINGERS.
DON'T GET BURNED.

P.S. AND TO WASH IT ALL DOWN

Parents might enjoy a chilled dry white wine or some
icy cold beer. For the younger cooks and picnickers, well,
a thermos of Shivering Cold Lemonade (the recipe is on
page 110) would be just right for summer picnics.

P.P.S. HOW TO TURN THE FISHERMEN'S PICNIC BASKET INTO A SKATERS' OR A SKIERS' OR A TOBOGGANERS' PICNIC BASKET . . . ANY OLD KIND OF PICNIC BASKET

Picnics are all-year-round Happy Days. You can switch
from fish to steak. Or perhaps your family likes to cut a
hole in the ice at the skating pond in the hope that some
hungry fish will nibble at the bait. As long as you can
build a campfire or take along a grill you're all set. Instead of the corn, take along a little coleslaw or some
apples or oranges. And if it's cold, cold, cold, take along a
big thermos of Chocolate Survival Kit (the recipe's on
page 137) to keep everyone warm. Parents might like to
add a jigger or two of rum to their Survival Kit.

Have fun!

GOURMET

COOKING

AND

MENUS

SEVEN

SO NOW YOU'RE
A JUNIOR GOURMET

A BAKER'S DOZEN
OF
GOURMET RECIPES

If you look it up in the dictionary, you'll learn that a gourmet is a connoisseur in eating. And if you look up connoisseur, you'll learn that it's a person who understands the details, techniques and principles of an art and is competent to act as a critical judge.

By now, that description ought to fit you. If you've cooked your way this far, you certainly understand a great deal about the details and techniques and principles of cooking. So here are some recipes in the classic tradition of great cookery for you to try out. Once you've completed these, you're ready to go on to really complicated sophisticated dishes. I'm proud of you.

THE ARMADILLO VEGETABLE

I'm sure you know which one this is. It's the artichoke. Did you ever see a vegetable that had such a coat of armor? But it's well worth the little trouble that it takes. Artichokes are one of the world's most elegant vegetables.

You'll need:

> 1 artichoke for each person
> Vinegar
> 1 teaspoon salt

1. Soak the artichoke in cold water with a couple of drops of vinegar in it for about 20 minutes.

2. Get a sharp knife. ARTICHOKES ARE TOUGH AND KNIVES CAN SLIP, SO PLEASE BE CAREFUL WITH THIS OPERATION. ASK A PARENT TO STAND BY. Cut off the stem as close as you can to the leaves at the bottom.

3. Cut off about an inch or two inches of the top of the artichoke. It all depends on how big it is. ASK YOUR MOTHER IF YOU'RE NOT SURE.

4. Pull off any tough or broken leaves around the stem end.

5. With a pair of kitchen scissors, go snip snip snip and cut off the prickly top of each artichoke leaf.

6. Put about 2 or 3 inches of water in a pan and let it boil. Add 2 tablespoons of vinegar. Put your artichokes in the water and cover the pan.

7. Depending on their size, they'll take from half an hour to 45 minutes to cook. They're done when you can pull off one of the leaves very easily. CAREFUL. DON'T BURN YOURSELF.

8. Let the cooked artichokes drain upside down.

9. When they're drained, place them right side up on salad plates and serve them with a little side dish of Green and Yellow Sauce on page 97 or the oil and vinegar dressing in Basic Salad Kit (that's on page 88).

LOVABLE ASPARAGUS

I suppose there are some people who don't like fresh asparagus. But I never met them.

You'll need:

(Well, it depends on how many people you have to feed. One pound of asparagus is enough for three people.)

> 1 pound of fresh asparagus
> Salt
> Butter

1. Wash the asparagus very carefully in cold water. I usually use my swivel-blade peeler on the stalks and scrape off all those scales, because sand and dirt often hide behind them. And sandy asparagus is not exactly gourmet fare.

2. Snap the stalks. You'll find that they break just naturally at the right place—just between the tender and the tough parts. Throw away the tough part.

3. Fill a shallow pan, big enough for the asparagus to lie on their sides, with about an inch of water. Or fill the top part of a double boiler with a few inches of water. When the water boils, add a little salt—about a teaspoonful—and lay the stalks on their sides or stand them up on their ends depending on which kind of pan you chose.

4. Cover the pan and let the asparagus cook until they are tender. This depends on their size, but 10 to 15 minutes should do it.

5. Drain them, spread a little butter over them and serve them quickly while they're hot.

NOTE ONE: These are very good with Veal Chops in an Envelope. (You'll learn how to make that on page 179.)

NOTE TWO: Italian gourmets like their asparagus with freshly grated Parmesan cheese sprinkled over the top. Try it. It's really good.

NOTE THREE: And, of course, you can serve asparagus cold. Serve it with the oil and vinegar sauce you learned to make in Basic Salad Kit (that's on page 88).

RICE WITH AN ITALIAN ACCENT

Next to spaghetti and macaroni, rice may be the most popular food in Italy. This way of cooking rice is easy. And the taste! I think you'll like it. Italians call this risotto.

You'll need:

    4 tablespoons of butter
    2 onions
    1 cup of rice
    2 cups of chicken broth (Perhaps you have some
        left over from Basic Chicken Soup. If not,
        use canned chicken broth)

1. Put the butter in a heavy pan or enamel-coated iron casserole. Turn the heat on low.

2. Peel the onions and chop them.

3. Cook the onions in the butter until they are almost transparent.

4. Now add the rice. Stir it around for about 4 or 5 minutes. It may get just a little brown.

5. Heat the chicken broth so that it's just ready to boil and then pour it in the casserole over the rice and onions.

6. Turn the oven on to 350 degrees. Cover the casserole and pop it in the oven. It will be done in half an hour.

7. Stir up the rice.

NOTE ONE: Some people think that this risotto plus a green salad or tomato salad is a very good meal all by itself. I'm one of those people.

NOTE TWO: Risotto goes well with Chicken Chunks (page 77) and Veal Chops in an Envelope (below) and Grate Chicken (page 103) and Caveman Steak (page 104). And that's just a start. Can you think of other things that go well with risotto?

NOTE THREE: You can add bits of chicken or ham or green pepper or tomatoes or sautéed chicken livers or lobster to risotto. Use your gourmet's imagination to create your very own version.

NOTE FOUR: Serve your risotto with a lot of grated Parmesan cheese.

VEAL CHOPS IN AN ENVELOPE

This is a very old French recipe. Nobody knows where it came from, but it's mentioned in French history books. The chops, along with herbs and seasonings, are sealed in a piece of paper before they're cooked. That keeps all the good flavor from escaping. And when you open the paper —oh my goodness, it smells delicious!

You'll need:

6 veal chops (Good veal is expensive, but these chops should be cut very thin, so it's not too extravagant a dish.)

¼ cup of olive oil (You could use corn oil, but you'd miss a little of the good flavor)

2 teaspoons of chopped parsley

2 teaspoons of finely chopped onion

2 teaspoons of chopped chives (If you can't buy fresh chives because they're out of season, try to find the frozen ones. And if you can't find the frozen ones, chop another teaspoon of onion.)

4 mushrooms, finely chopped (Wash them quickly first. Pat them dry on a paper towel. Cut off the stems. If you want, you can peel the mushrooms, but you don't have to.)

Salt

Pepper (Ground by hand, naturally.)

Parchment paper (I know you probably don't have any parchment paper. Here's what you can use: very good heavy white paper. The kind you would type a novel on. Or write an invitation on.)

Butter

(You have to start making this recipe the morning of the day you're going to serve the chops. Or even the night before. But don't worry, this is one of the easiest recipes you've ever put together.)

1. Put the chops on a shallow platter and pour the olive oil over them. Let them soak up the olive oil for 12 hours. Turn them once in a while. If you leave them for 16 hours, that's okay.

2. Put your chopped parsley, onion, chives and mush-

rooms all together in a little bowl. Stir them around with a fork to mix them.

3. Now put each chop in the center of a piece of your very, very best white paper.

4. Smear a little butter over each side of the chops, then put some of your mixed herbs on top of each chop. Pat the herbs down into the butter, then turn the chops over and put some more herb mixture on the other side.

5. Sprinkle a little salt and grind a little pepper over each chop. Not much. Just a little.

6. Now fold the paper over the chop very carefully. Seal it with Scotch tape. Try to seal each chop securely so no good flavor can escape until you're ready.

7. Turn the oven on to 300 degrees.

8. Put all your little paper packages into a roasting pan and put them in the oven for 35 minutes.

9. That's all there is to it. After 35 minutes, take the pan out of the oven. Transfer the paper packages to a serving platter. Each person gets a chop that's still all wrapped up.

NOTE: It's a good idea to give everyone a little extra dish to put his paper wrapping in.

BEEF WITH A RUSSIAN ACCENT

The Russian accent here is sour cream and mushrooms. Actually, this dish has a name of its own. It's called Beef Stroganoff. Many hostesses serve Beef Stroganoff at dinner parties. When you make it, you'll understand why.

You'll need:

2 pounds of tenderloin of beef (Tenderloin is
extremely expensive. If you want, you can
use sirloin. It tastes every bit as good even
though it's not quite traditional.)
1 tablespoon of finely chopped onion
4 tablespoons of butter
½ pound of mushrooms
Salt
1 cup of sour cream

1. Wash your hands, tie on your apron and choose a good sharp knife. DON'T BE CARELESS. WATCH WHAT YOU'RE DOING. Cut the beef in thin strips, about one inch wide and, oh, about 2½ inches long.

2. Melt 2 tablespoons of butter in your big black frying pan and cook the chopped onion in it for 1 minute.

3. Add the beef to the butter and onion. Keep stirring it so that it will get brown all over. Cook it for 5 minutes and then take the pan off the stove.

4. Wash the mushrooms quickly, just run water over them. Snap off the stems. And slice the mushroom caps.

5. Melt the other 2 tablespoons of butter in a small frying pan. Add the sliced mushrooms. Let the mushrooms cook for 5 minutes. Stir them when you think it's necessary.

6. Sprinkle the mushrooms with just a little salt and stir them around once more.

7. Add the mushrooms to the browned beef.

8. Add the sour cream to the mushrooms and beef. Stir everything around to mix it, then put the pan back on the stove until the sour cream is warmed.

9. Taste the sour cream sauce. Does it need a little salt? Some people think a tiny bit of grated nutmeg is good. All right, that's it.

10. Serve Beef Stoganoff with rice—white rice or brown rice.

FLAKY PIE CRUST

In the olden days, they used to say a good cook has "a light hand with pie crust." Now people buy factory-made pie crust at the frozen food counter. It's a shame, because they don't know what they're missing. Once you get the knack of it, making pie crust is as easy as pie. In fact, that's where the saying came from.

You'll need:

    2 cups of flour
    1 teaspoon of salt
    ⅔ cup of lard
    4 to 5 tablespoons of ice water. (Just put a
        cup of cold water and a few ice cubes in
        a small bowl, then measure out the water
        as needed.)

1. Wash your hands. Then sift the 2 cups of flour and the salt into a mixing bowl.

2. Take two knives or a pastry blender and mix in the lard. The lard should have come straight out of the refrigerator and be very cold. ASK YOUR MOTHER TO SHOW YOU HOW TO USE THE TWO KNIVES SO THAT YOU CUT THE LARD INTO SMALL PIECES THAT LOOK LIKE CORNMEAL OR GRAPE-NUTS. You should work very quickly to get the whole thing mixed up. Remember, don't mash the lard, cut it. The faster you work the better.

3. When it all looks something like Grape-Nuts, sprinkle

a tablespoon of water over the pastry and stir it in with a blending fork.

4. Then sprinkle a second tablespoon of ice water over the pastry and stir that in with a blending fork.

5. Continue until enough water has been added so that you can shape the dough into a ball that holds together. It will come away from the side of the bowl as you stir it. You may not need all 5 tablespoons of ice water.

6. The minute you can pat the dough into a ball, wrap it up in plastic wrap or aluminum foil and put it in the refrigerator. Handle it as little as possible. Let it sit in the refrigerator for half an hour at least. You can leave it in for a day, or even two, if you've wrapped it very carefully so no air can get at it.

7. This is the time to prepare the filling. My favorite apple pie recipe is on page 190. But you can make a cherry pie or a blueberry pie or just about any kind you like. And you can use this crust to make Cheese and Onion Pie. It's the next recipe. YOU MIGHT WANT TO ASK YOUR MOTHER TO PREPARE THE FILLING WHILE YOU MAKE THE PIE CRUST. OR VICE VERSA. DO YOU KNOW WHAT VICE VERSA MEANS? IF YOU DON'T, YOU'D BETTER LOOK IT UP IN THE DICTIONARY.

8. When the filling is prepared, it's time to roll out the pie crust. Get out a 9-inch pie plate. If your mother has a pastry board, put a little flour on it—and some on your rolling pin. ASK YOUR MOTHER WHERE YOU SHOULD ROLL OUT THE PIE CRUST.

9. Take the dough out of the refrigerator. Divide it in half. Put half on your working surface and stick the other half back in the refrigerator until you need it.

10. Flatten the dough with the heel of your hand and then start rolling it out. This is fun, but you may have trouble the first time. Don't worry. You'll soon get the knack and then it will truly be "as easy as pie." YOUR MOTHER CAN HELP YOU IF THINGS GET TOO STICKY.

11. Start rolling from the center out. Remember what I said about a light hand. Make your rolling light and fast. Don't bear down hard on the rolling pin. Keep rolling from the center out, but roll in a different direction each time. You have to make a circle of pastry that's about 11 inches in diameter. And it should be about ⅛ inch thick.

12. You won't be able to make a perfect circle. Perhaps you'll make a very funny shape the first time. Don't worry. You can cut off a piece of the crust and stick it on where you need it. Here's what you do. Just wet the edge of your pastry "patch" with cold water and stick it where it will do the most good. Here's a trick to remember: If you want, roll out the pastry between two pieces of wax paper. That way, it can't stick to your rolling pin.

13. When the crust looks about the right shape, pick up one side very carefully and fold it over the other half to make a half circle.

14. Now, very carefully again, pick up the crust and put it in the pie plate. It should cover half the plate. Unfold it to cover the rest of the plate.

15. Be very gentle now. Fit the crust into the plate and push it around the sides so there's no air underneath the crust.

16. Some of the crust may hang over the edge of the pie plate. Cut it off with a knife that you dipped in cold water. ASK YOUR MOTHER TO HELP YOU. Maybe

you'll need to make a couple more "patches" this first time.

17. Now you are ready to add your filling.

CHEESE AND ONION PIE

In France, this is called Quiche (it's pronounced keesh) Lorraine. Lorraine is the name of the French province where the dish originated. It's a pie crust with a cheesy filling. This recipe is a good example of how all the things you learn work together to make rather complicated dishes. For instance, this calls for Flaky Pie Crust, for fried bacon (and that was the very first recipe in this book) and for a custard sauce that's similar to the one you made in the ice cream recipe. You don't have to keep stirring this one over hot water; it cooks quietly in the pie crust. But the principle is the same: Milk and eggs cook together to make a thick sauce.

You'll need:

    1 pie crust for a 9-inch pie plate (That's half the Flaky Pie Crust recipe.)

    4 slices of bacon

    1 tablespoon of butter

    ½ cup of chopped scallions (Just use the green parts. You could use the white if you absolutely had to, but the green is more attractive in the finished dish.)

    ½ pound of imported Swiss cheese (If the imported kind is too expensive, American Swiss can be used. It's very good; it's just not quite authentic. But I wouldn't waste time worrying about that.)

    3 eggs

    2 cups of milk

Grated nutmeg (If your mother has a whole nutmeg and a tiny nutmeg grater, use it. It will make a lot of difference in the flavor in this particular recipe. Otherwise, use the grated nutmeg from the little spice tin.)

1. All right. Wash your hands and let's get started. Fit the pie crust into the pie plate. Turn the oven on to 450 degrees. And when it reaches 450, pop the pie crust into the oven for 4 or 5 minutes. Then take it out and let it cool in the pie plate on a wire rack.

2. Cook the bacon until it's crispy and brown. (Turn back to the recipes for Alarm Clock Bacon on page 27 if you think you need careful directions.) Drain the cooked bacon on paper towels. When it's dry, crumble it into little pieces and put it aside for the moment.

3. Melt the butter in the frying pan and add the chopped green scallions. Let them cook over low heat for 5 minutes. Stir them occasionally so they won't stick to the pan.

4. Grate the Swiss cheese with the coarse side of the grater. Or, if you want, you can chop it into small cubes. Do whichever you feel like. JUST WATCH YOUR FINGERS WHILE YOU'RE DOING IT.

5. Break the eggs into a bowl and beat them with a fork or a whisk for a minute. Pour the 2 cups of milk into the eggs and stir to mix.

6. Now you put it all together. Sprinkle the bacon bits over the bottom of the pie crust. Then spoon the cooked scallions over the bacon bits. Last of all, add the grated cheese.

7. Now, carefully, pour the milk and eggs into the pie crust.

8. Grate a little nutmeg over the top.

9. Tuck your quiche into the oven. It should cook at 450 degrees for 10 minutes.

10. After 10 minutes, turn the heat down to 325 degrees and let the quiche cook for 20 minutes. When it's done, it should be firm. The custard should not be wiggly.

GOOD IDEA ONE: Serve this for lunch or supper, with a tossed green salad.

GOOD IDEA TWO: Fit your pie crust into cupcake tins instead of a pie plate and make individual little cheese and onion tarts. They don't need to cook as long, about 8 minutes at 450 degrees and 10 to 12 at 325 degrees.

GOOD IDEA THREE: Use cut-up ham instead of bacon.

LIGHT AS A FEATHER CHEESE SOUFFLÉ

Soufflé is a French word for a very light and airy dish made with eggs. A soufflé can be a first course for a very special dinner or a main course and a sweet one can be a super-elegant dessert.

Some people think soufflés are hard to make. Don't you believe it.

You'll need:

> 1 cup of milk
> 3 tablespoons of butter
> 3 tablespoons of flour
> 1 teaspoon of salt
> 1 cup of grated Cheddar cheese (Buy the cheese in a chunk and grate it yourself. It's well worth the extra effort.)
> 4 eggs

(A soufflé is really nothing but a cream sauce—the same kind of sauce you made for Glop on Toast and for Macaroni and You-Know-What—with beaten egg whites folded into it to make it light and fluffy.)

1. Scald the milk. Heat it until it is just on the point of boiling, then take it off the stove.

2. Melt the butter in the top of a double boiler or in a thick-bottomed saucepan.

3. When the butter is melted, stir in the flour with your wooden spoon. Keep stirring it for a minute or so, then take it off the heat.

4. Pour the scalded milk into the butter and flour mixture very slowly. Add the salt. Keep stirring all the time. As soon as all the milk is mixed in, put the pan back on the heat and keep stirring until the sauce is completely smooth and thickened. You'll notice as you stir that it gets thicker and thicker. Then take it off the heat and add the cheese. Keep stirring until the cheese is melted.

5. Turn the oven on to 375 degrees.

6. Break the eggs and separate the whites and yolks. CAREFUL NOW. The main thing is not to get any yolk in the whites, because then they won't beat up as well. IF YOU'RE HAVING TROUBLE, ASK YOUR MOTHER TO HELP. But you really shouldn't worry if you mess up a couple of eggs; you can always use them for scrambled eggs tomorrow morning.

7. Beat the yolks with your rotary egg beater (NOT the electric mixer) until they are quite pale and lemony colored.

8. Then pour the cooled cream sauce mixture into the egg yolks, little by little. The sauce should be quite cool, otherwise it will cook the yolks and you'll be in trouble.

9. Now, wash off the egg beater and beat the egg whites. Keep beating them until they are very stiff and shiny.

10. Fold half of the egg-white mixture into the cream sauce and egg-yolk mixture. Remember how you fold? With the rubber spatula? (If you don't, turn back to the Once-Upon-a-Birthday Cake recipe on page 141.) Fold the whites in pretty well.

11. Now fold the other half of the egg whites in. But these should not be mixed in as well. Just fold them in until they are slightly mixed in.

12. Butter a soufflé dish. This is a straight-sided white porcelain dish. If your mother doesn't have one, use a casserole with straight sides. Pour your mixture into the buttered soufflé dish and pop it into the oven for 35 minutes. Don't jump up and down in the kitchen while your soufflé is cooking or it will fall. Just be nice and quiet.

13. Open the oven door gently after 35 minutes. The soufflé should be all puffed up and a toasty golden brown color. It's ready to serve this very minute. If you don't eat it right off, the soufflé will fall. It will still taste good, but it will be a sorry sight.

NEW ENGLAND APPLE PIE

It's full of sugar and spice and everything nice. And it's proof that gourmet cooking doesn't necessarily mean French cooking.

You'll need:

    2 pounds of apples
    ¾ cup of sugar

1 teaspoon of cinnamon
½ teaspoon of powdered cloves
½ teaspoon of nutmeg (Grate it yourself if your
    mother has a nutmeg grater.)
½ teaspoon of salt
½ lemon
2 tablespoons of butter
2 pie crusts (Just follow the recipe for Flaky
    Pie Crust on page 183.)

1. Turn the oven on to 450 degrees.

2. Peel the apples (PLEASE, BE CAREFUL.) Cut them in quarters, then cut out the cores. Now slice the quarters evenly. Put the apple slices into a large bowl. You'll have about 6 cups of apple slices.

3. Squeeze the lemon and sprinkle the lemon juice over the apple slices.

4. Mix the sugar, cinnamon, powdered cloves, nutmeg and salt together in a bowl.

5. Grate the rind of the half lemon and add that to the sugar and spice bowl.

6. Line a 9-inch pie plate with your pie crust and then the fun begins. Start filling the pie plate with the apple slices. Arrange them carefully in circles. When the bottom of the crust is covered, sprinkle some of the sugar and spice mixture over it. Then make another neat layer of apple slices and sprinkle more sugar and spice over it. Keep on doing this until you've used up all the apple slices. At the very end, make an extra couple of rows of apple slices in the very middle of the pie so that it will be higher in the middle than on the edges.

7. Now break the butter up into little bits and dot it all over the top of the apples. Sprinkle the rest of the sugar

and spice mixture over the apple slices. If there's a little lemon juice left in the bowl that held the apples, pour that over the apple slices, too.

8. Now place the top crust on your pie. Moisten the edge of the bottom crust with ice water and then with your thumbs press the top crust down on it all the way around the rim. This makes a pretty design and seals the crusts together so that no juice will get out. Some people use a fork to press the edges together. And that makes a nice design, too. And use the fork to prick holes in the crust so the steam can escape. YOUR MOTHER MAY HAVE HER OWN WAY OF DOING THIS. ASK HER TO SHOW YOU.

9. Your pie is ready to bake. An apple pie should be baked at 450 degrees for 40 minutes. It's a good idea to put a piece of aluminum foil in the bottom of the oven right under the pie—just in case some of the juice escapes. This way the oven won't get dirty.

STRAWBERRIES ROMANOFF

One of the most famous cooks in the world was a Frenchman named August Escoffier. He was called "the king of chefs and the chef of kings." One of his cookbooks contained 2,984 recipes. And some of them were so complicated they took as much as a week to prepare.

But this recipe, which is adapted from one of Escoffier's, is simple and quick. It shows that gourmet cooking does not have to be complicated. It's partly a matter of putting flavors and textures together so that the result . . . well, try this recipe and see what you think of the result. You'll need:

1 pint of ripe, red, juicy strawberries
½ cup of fresh squeezed orange juice
Whipped cream

1. Hull the strawberries, that is, take off the stem and the green part at the top. Use your fingers. Make sure that every strawberry is perfect and ripe.

2. Put the strawberries in a bowl and pour the fresh orange juice over them half an hour before you want to serve them. Stir them around with a fork a couple of times.

3. Place your strawberries in champagne glasses. Spoon a little of the juice into each glass. And top each glass of strawberries with your whipped cream.

NOTE: You see how simple this is? But it took a gourmet to think of putting strawberries and orange juice together and covering it with whipped cream. Escoffier's version calls for a little curaçao in the orange juice. But that's expensive. And you don't need to be that much of a gourmet at your age.

SOMETHING TO THINK ABOUT

If you were to serve Beef Stroganoff (page 181) and Strawberries Romanoff at the same meal, it would be too much of a good thing. Why? Because the beef is swimming in a sour cream sauce and the strawberries sit under a mountain of whipped cream. A gourmet might serve strawberries *without* whipped cream, if he were having Beef Stroganoff for dinner.

MERINGUES

Meringues are nothing but egg whites and sugar whipped together and baked slowly. Nothing but? Nothing but delicious. As far as anyone can tell, they were invented in 1720. Some people say an Italian invented them; others that it was a Swiss, and still other people say a German invented them. But there are two things that we know for certain. Marie Antoinette (Do you know who she was? If not, ask your mother or father.) used to go out into the palace kitchen and make them with her royal hands. And a very famous cook, whose name, interestingly enough, was Marie Antonin (that's awfully close to Marie Antoinette) Carême, used to decorate many of his fancy desserts with them. Carême was a fascinating man. At one time he cooked for Napoleon. Carême's family was very poor and he was one of twenty-five children. No wonder he got interested in food. I think you'll be interested in these meringues.

You'll need:

> 2 egg whites (The eggs should be a couple of
> days old, so don't rush around trying to get
> newly laid eggs. And the whites should be
> at room temperature.)
> 8 tablespoons of sugar
> 1 teaspoon of vanilla

1. Cover a cooky sheet with brown paper.
2. Turn the oven on to 250 degrees.
3. Start beating your egg whites. You can use an electric mixer or the rotary egg beater.
4. When the whites are very stiff and look dry, start

beating in the sugar. Add 1 tablespoon at a time and beat it in well before you add the next tablespoon of sugar. Beat in 6 tablespoons of sugar and keep on beating until the sugar and egg mixture holds its shape when you lift up a spoonful.

5. Now add the vanilla.

6. You have 2 tablespoons of sugar left. Fold them into the mixture very carefully with your rubber spatula. Use the folding motion.

7. If you have a pastry bag, put the meringue mixture in it. Then squirt it out on the brown paper covering the cooky sheet in rings that are about 3 inches in diameter. Or you can just place spoonfuls of meringue on the paper.

8. Bake for 50 minutes, then take them out of the oven. As soon as you can touch the meringues without getting burned, take the paper off them. It will probably stick, so moisten the bottom of the paper—just a little—with cold water. Just rub your wet finger across the paper. That will help it come loose.

NOTE ONE: You can fill these meringues with whipped cream or ice cream. For a really glorious dessert, fill them with Strawberries Romanoff. That's worthy of royalty. Don't you agree?

NOTE TWO: If you fill the meringues with ice cream, pour Superchocolate Nut Sauce (page 197) over each one. Yummy.

ICE CREAM WHIRLIGIG

This is a dessert that your friends won't believe you made yourself. It looks fantastically professional. But there's nothing to it that you don't know how to do already, if you've cooked your way through the preceding chapters. It's just a matter of using your knowledge.

You'll need:

> 1 recipe for Once-Upon-a-Birthday Cake (That's on page 141.)
> Confectioners' sugar
> 1 pint of vanilla ice cream (If you have all the time in the world on your hands, well, I'd suggest you make Cranky Ice Cream (page 145). But if you have other things to do, just buy the best ice cream you can find.)
> 1 pint of chocolate or strawberry ice cream (The same goes for this.)

1. Turn the oven on to 350 degrees.

2. Butter a jelly-roll pan. It should be about 10 by 14 inches. Then line the pan with wax paper and butter the wax paper. You don't want to take a chance of the cake sticking.

3. Pour the cake batter into the jelly-roll pan. If there's any left over, why don't you make a few cupcakes?

4. Place it in the oven and let it bake for about 12 minutes. It should be firm; don't let it bake too long or it will be too dry.

5. While the cake is baking, spread a clean dish towel out on the kitchen table or counter. Sprinkle confectioners' sugar all over the dish towel.

6. When the cake is done, turn the jelly-roll pan upside down on the sugar-covered dish towel. When the cake comes out, don't waste a second. Start pulling the wax paper off. CAREFUL!

7. Take a look at your cake. Are the edges very brown and crusty? If they are, you'll have to cut them off. Use a

sharp knife. Be neat. And don't cut off any more than you have to. Okay, go ahead, eat the cut-off pieces.

8. Now, use both hands and roll up the cake. Easy does it. Be very gentle. When it's rolled, wrap the dish towel around it and let it rest until you're almost ready to serve it.

9. About 15 minutes before you're ready to serve your Ice Cream Whirligig take the 2 pints of ice cream out of the refrigerator and let them get slightly soft.

10. Unroll your cake. Spread the soft vanilla ice cream over it.

11. Now spread the chocolate or strawberry ice cream over the vanilla. Spread it as evenly as you can, but it doesn't have to be perfect.

12. Now roll it up again. And serve it. You should hear a lot of exclamations.

NOTE ONE: Whirligig can be varied in many ways. You can use different flavors of ice cream. Or you can fill it with whipped cream instead of ice cream.

NOTE TWO: Perhaps you would like to turn the Whirligig into an old-fashioned jelly roll. Nothing could be easier. Just spread the cake with raspberry jam or currant jelly and roll it up. Sprinkle the top of the roll with more confectioners' sugar. Delicious!

NOTE THREE: Serve Ice Cream Whirligig with Superchocolate Nut Sauce. That's the last word in great desserts. (It's the last recipe in this book, too.)

SUPERCHOCOLATE NUT SAUCE

If you like chocolate sauce on vanilla ice cream, well—here's a super sauce.

You'll need:

> ½ cup of butter (That's one stick.)
> 2 cups of chopped walnuts
> 2 cups of semi-sweet chocolate bits

1. Get out your big frying pan, turn the heat on to medium-low and melt the butter.

2. Add the walnuts to the melted butter and keep stirring until the nuts are slightly browned. Take the frying pan off the heat.

3. Add the chocolate bits to the butter and nuts. Stir until the chocolate is melted. And that's it.

NOTE: If you're not going to use the sauce immediately, keep it warm over hot water until you're ready for it.

PUTTING

IT

ALL

TOGETHER

EIGHT

A BAKER'S DOZEN
of
COOKALONG MENUS

What goes with what? What makes a perfect meal? Now that you've become an accomplished and creative cook, your opinion is as good as anyone's. You know by now that every course should have something new to offer—in taste, in color, in texture. Who wants a meal of white boiled chicken, white rice and vanilla ice cream? Just think how much better toasty golden baked chicken, a lettuce and tomato salad and vanilla ice cream with a few fresh strawberries would taste—and look.

Here's a baker's dozen of menus, using the dishes you have learned to make in your cookalong sessions, to get you started on your menu planning. Perhaps you'll want to make some changes. That's fine. What's important is your taste and your idea of what should go with what.

This baker's dozen of menus make good cookalong projects. There are menus here for every degree of competence. You and your father (or your sister or brother) can surprise Mother with breakfast in bed some morning. The Week Night Supper for the Family is within the abilities of the beginner cook. And if Junior and Senior Cooks collaborate, the All-American Sunday Dinner or Cold-Weather Saturday Night Supper, New England Style are easy enough to prepare—and fun.

A SUNDAY BREAKFAST

Fresh Strawberries in Orange Juice
Parlez-Vous French Toast   Maple Syrup
Alarm Clock Bacon
Chocolate Survival Kit

LET'S SURPRISE MOTHER WITH BREAKFAST IN BED

Orange Juice
(And please squeeze it yourself. Freshly squeezed orange juice tastes so much better than canned or frozen juice.)
Friendly Eggs   Alarm Clock Bacon
Toast   Jam or Marmalade
Coffee or Tea
(Which does she prefer?)

AN ALL-AMERICAN SUNDAY DINNER

Hot Buttered Juice
Basic Roast Beef
Fancy Baked Potatoes   Good Old Spinach
Cranky Vanilla Ice Cream
with
Superchocolate Nut Sauce

A WEEK NIGHT SUPPER FOR THE FAMILY

Katy's Throw-Everything-In Meat Loaf
Green Salad
Flying Saucer Pancake

A GOOD COMPANY DINNER

(Maybe your grandparents are visiting or your
favorite aunt and uncle.)
The Armadillo Vegetable
(Serve the artichokes cold with an oil and vinegar
sauce.)
Holiday Bird
Skinny Potatoes   Green Salad
Raspberry Jam Jelly Roll
(See Note Two at the end of Ice Cream Whirligig)

A GOURMET FEAST

Lovable Asparagus
(Serve the asparagus cold with an oil and vinegar
dressing. This looks especially good if you sprinkle
chopped parsley and chives over the asparagus.)
Veal Chops in an Envelope
Rice
Strawberries Romanoff in Meringue Shells

A BUFFET SUPPER

Third-Generation Lasagne
Crusty Italian Bread and Bread Sticks
Green Salad with Tomatoes and Scallions
A Big Bowl of Apples and Pears and Tangerines

A COLD-WEATHER SATURDAY NIGHT SUPPER, NEW ENGLAND STYLE

Historical Beans
Johnnycake
Green Salad
Cornflake Cake with Whipped Cream

WHEN IT'S 90 DEGREES IN THE SHADE

Billion-Dollar Lobster Roll
with
Sliced Tomatoes
Sixteen-Minute Blueberry Cheesecake
Shivering Cold Lemonade

THE TEAM'S COMING OVER FOR A COOKOUT

Caveman Steak
Potato Salad
Crusty, Buttered French Bread
New England Apple Pie

ALL MY BEST FRIENDS ARE COMING
FOR A SLUMBER PARTY

Slumber Party Supper
Susan's French Beef Stew
Crusty French Bread   Basic Green Salad
Ice Cream Whirligig

A Midnight (and Later) Snack
*Even if you've been eating all evening, you'll prob-
ably be hungry before you decide to go to sleep.
Here's a snack to keep you from starving to death
before breakfast.*

Phony Pizza
Apples and Gingerbread Men

A Brunch for the Morning After
Grapefruit or Orange Segments
Free-Style Pancakes*   Maple Syrup
Alarm Clock Bacon
Chocolate Survival Kit

* Mix up a couple of bowls of basic pancake batter. Then put
out a choice of goodies to mix in with the pancakes. For instance,
some cut-up ham, some cranberries, blueberries, apple chunks. Use
your imagination. Your friends will have a good time making their
individual pancakes.

THE END

Good-bye. I hate to say it. All the time I've been working on *The Cookalong Book* I've felt as if I were talking and working with you. And now I'm going to miss you.

I hope that when you, the Junior Cook, have a home of your own, you'll still have this book. Perhaps you'll put it on the cookbook shelf in your own kitchen—wherever that will be. That seems a long time away, doesn't it? But it isn't really. I'd like to think that you'll want to cook with your own children from your old *Cookalong Book.* Perhaps you'll tell them stories about your picnics and parties and the things you liked to cook best.

And to my co-worker, the Senior Cook, I hope that you, too, enjoyed the sharing of time and work and ideas and love.

Anyway, I feel as if we're friends now. I hope you feel the same way. Good-bye.

INDEX

Apple
Lollypops, 133–134
Pie, New England, 190–192
Sandwiches, 69–70
Armadillo Vegetable, The, 176–177
Artichoke, 176–177
Asparagus, Lovable, 177–178

Bacon, 27–29
Lettuce and Tomato, 54–55
Basic
Chicken Soup, 59–62
Flapjacks, 33–35
Roast Beef, 84–86
Salad Kit, Beginners, 88–90
Spaghetti, 73–74
Beans
Historical, 124–125
Wild West, 126–127
Beginner's Basic Salad Kit, 88–90
Ben's Eatemallup Muffins, 39–41
Beef
Basic Roast, 84–86
Boilaway, 120–122

Caveman Steak, 104–105
Chipped, on Toast, 48–50
Roast, in Ketchup Sandwiches, 69
with a Russian Accent, 181–183
Second-Helping Pot Roast, 81–84
Stew, Susan's French, 79–81
Stroganoff, 181–183
Billion-Dollar Lobster Rolls, 98–100
BLT on Toast, 54–55
Blueberry Cheesecake, Sixteen-Minute, 107–109
Boilaway Beef, 120–122
Boiled Ham, 68–69
Bread
Ginger
Men and Women and Stars and Wreaths, et cetera, 152–156
Spicy, 130–132
Muscleman, 111–117
Buttered Juice, Hot, 92

Cake(s)
Cornflake, 41–44

Johnny-, 127–128
Once-Upon-a-Birthday, 141–145
Sixteen-Minute Blueberry Cheese-, 107–109
Campfire Potatoes, 169–170
Candy
Pully-Tuggy Taffy, 134–136
Casserole, Canny, 57–59
Caveman Steak, 104–105
Chanukah Seedy Cookies, 149–150
Cheese
in Apple Sandwiches, 69–70
Balls, Green, 157–159
Macaroni and, 52–54
and Onion Pie, 186–188
Soufflé, Light as a Feather, 188–190
Cheesecake, Sixteen-Minute Blueberry, 107–109
Chicken
Chunks, Sam's, 77–78
Grate, 103
Holiday Bird, 165–167
Salad, Sally's Prize-Winning, 62–64
Soup, Basic, 59–62
Chipped Beef on Toast, 48–50
Chocolate
Survival Kit, 137–138
Super-, Nut Sauce, 197–198

Chops, Veal, in an Envelope, 179–181
Cookies, Chanukah Seedy, 149–150
Corn, Foiled Again, 171–172
Cornflake Cake, 41–44
Cranky Ice Cream, 145–147
Cream
Sauce for Glop on Toast, 49–50
Whipped, 132–133
Crust, Pie
Crumbly, 109
Flaky, 183–186

Diet Lunches, 68–70
Dippy Shrimp, 100–101

Eggs, Scrambled, 29–31
Energy Special, 66–67

Fancy Baked Potatoes, 87–88
First Catch Your Fish, 168–169
Fish
First Catch Your, 168–169
Tuna, Casserole, 57–59
Fishermen's Picnic Basket, 167
Flaky Pie Crust, 183–186

Flapjacks
Basic, 33–35
Fruity, 35–36
Flying Saucer Pancake, 37–39
Foiled Again Corn, 171–172
Frankfurters, in Ken's Double Feature, 56–57
French Toast, 31–32

Gingerbread
Men and Women and Stars and Wreaths, et cetera, 152–156
Spicy, 130–132
Glop on Toast, 48–50
Good Old Spinach, 90–92
Grate Chicken, 103
Green
Cheese Balls, 157–159
and Yellow Sauce, 97–98
Griddle Cakes, Meaty, 36–37

Ham, Boiled, 68–69
Hamburger, 56–57
Historical Beans, 124–125
Holiday Bird, 165–167
Hot
Buttered Juice, 92
and Cold Sauce, 123
Dogs, 56–57

Ice Cream
Cranky, 145–147
How to Freeze, 148–149
Snow Bowl, 136–137
Whirligig, 195–197

Jam, Your Own Homemade Strawberry, 117–119
Jeff's Messy Macroni, 72
Jelly Waffles, Peanut Butter and, 67–68
Johnnycake, 127–128
Juice, Hot Buttered, 92

Katy's Throw-Everything-in Meat Loaf, 78–79
Ken's Double Feature, 56–57
Ketchup Sandwiches, 69

Lasagne, Third Generation, 128–130
Lazy Lucy's Wake-up Rice, 46–48
Lemonade, Shivering Cold, 110–111
Light as a Feather Cheese Soufflé, 188–190
Linda's Diet Lunches, 68–70
Lobster
Roll, Billion-Dollar, 98–100
Spells Summer, 95–97
Lollypops, Apple, 133–134

Lovable Asparagus, 177–178

Macaroni
  Jeff's Messy, 72
  and You-Know-What, 52–54
Meatballs and Spaghetti, 75–77
Meat Loaf, Katy's Throw-Everything-in 78–79
Meaty Griddle Cakes, 36–37
Meringues, 194–195
Muffins
  Ben's Eatemallup, 39–41
  in Disguise, 41
  English, as Base for Phony Pizza, 55–56
Muscleman Bread, 111–117
Mustard Sandwiches, 68–69

New England Apple Pie, 190–192

Oatburgers, 45–46
Oatmeal, 44–45
Once-Upon-a-Birthday Cake, 141–145
Onion's Hooray! 170–171

Pancake(s), 33–39
  Basic Flapjacks, 33–35

Flying Saucer, 37–39
Fruity Flapjacks, 35–36
Meaty Griddle Cakes, 36–37
Pâté Maison, Your Own, 163–164
Peaches in a Basket, 159–163
Peanut Butter
  and Jelly Waffles, 67–68
  Sandwich, 66–67
Pete's Tower of Pisa, 101–102
Phony Pizza, 55–56
Pickled Buddy Sauce, 123
Pie
  Apple, New England, 190–192
  Cheese and Onion, 186–188
  Crust
    Crumbly, 109
    Flaky, 183–186
Pizza, Phony, 55–56
Popcorn Balls, 150–152
Potato(es)
  Baked, Fancy, 87–88
  Campfire, 169–170
  Salad, 105–107
  Skinny, 86–87
Pot Roast, Second-Helping, 81–84
Pully-Tuggy Taffy, 134–136

Quiche Lorraine, 186–188

Rice
　　with an Italian Accent, 178–
　　　　179
　　Lazy Lucy's Wake-up,
　　　　46–48
Roast
　　Beef
　　　　Basic, 84–86
　　　　in Ketchup Sandwiches,
　　　　　　69
　　　　Pot, Second-Helping, 81–84
Roll, Billion-Dollar Lobster,
　　98–100

Salad
　　Beginner's Basic Kit, 88–90
　　Chicken, 62–64
　　Potato, There's, 105–107
Sally's Prize-Winning
　　Chicken Salad, 62–64
Sam's Chicken Chunks, 77–
　　78
Sandwich(es)
　　Apple, 69–70
　　Energy Special, 66–67
　　Ketchup, 69
　　Mustard, 68–69
　　Pete's Tower of Pisa, 101–
　　　　102
Sauce
　　Cream, for Glop on Toast,
　　　　49–50
　　Green and Yellow, 97–98

Hot and Cold, 123
Pickled Buddy, 123
Superchocolate Nut, 197–
　　198
Second-Helping Pot Roast,
　　81–84
Shivering Cold Lemonade,
　　110–111
Shrimp, Dippy, 100–101
Sixteen-Minute Blueberry
　　Cheesecake, 107–
　　109
Skinny Potatoes, 86–87
Snow Bowl, 136–137
Soufflé, Cheese, Light as a
　　Feather, 188–190
Soup, Chicken, 59–62
Spaghetti
　　Basic, 73–74
　　and Meatballs, 75–77
Spicy Gingerbread, 130–
　　132
Spinach, Good Old, 90–92
Steak, Caveman, 104–105
Stew, Beef, Susan's French,
　　79–81
Strawberry(ies)
　　Jam, Your Own Homemade,
　　　　117–119
　　Romanoff, 192–193
Stroganoff, Beef, 181–183
Superchocolate Nut Sauce,
　　198

Susan's French Beef Stew, 79–81

Taffy, Pully-Tuggy, 134–136
There's Potato Salad, 105–107
Third-Generation Lasagne, 128–130
Toast, French, 31–32
Tomato Hideway, 64–65
Tuna Fish Casserole, 57–59

Veal Chops in an Envelope, 179–181

Waffles, Peanut Butter and Jelly, 67–68
Whipped Cream, 132–133
Wild West Beans, 126–127

Yellow and Green Sauce, 97–98
Your Own
    Homemade Strawberry Jam, 117–119
    Pâté Maison, 163–164